THE MAGNIFICENT FROLIC

The Magnificent Frolic

BY BARRY WOOD

The Westminster Press · Philadelphia

ISBN 0–664–24880–2

LIBRARY OF CONGRESS CATALOG CARD NO.
78–101698

PUBLISHED BY THE WESTMINSTER PRESS®
PHILADELPHIA, PENNSYLVANIA

PRINTED IN THE UNITED STATES OF AMERICA

To
Daisy Wood
and
Mildred Bell
companions of my youth

CONTENTS

PREFACE

The vast majority of people today live their lives as if there were no God. For this majority, the quiet Sunday gatherings across the nation seem like futile attempts to bring to life the God of a past age, the supernatural God who knows all things and loves all men. Today's sophisticated intellectual wants none of this. Yet many who have rejected the Divine Mechanic have nevertheless retained the machine—the fragmented universe of scientism, where man is a chemical fantasy, an aberration upon the stony surface of an indifferent universe. Defection from church-style religion has left a vacuum in the lives of many, and the postreligious activities that have rushed in are mechanical, repetitious, and shot through with futility and frustration. How else are we to regard the tiresome devotion to the stock market, mass-produced "culture," key clubs, grass, astrology, mindless TV, and the American Way of Life?

But somewhere between the cult of the Mechanic and devotion to the machine is a new conception of things, growing out of process philosophy, systems theory, field analysis, biological ecology, evolutionary studies, peak-experience psychology, and Oriental philosophy. Slowly it is becoming clear that the split-level universe of "Creator" and "creation" is untenable. For all is "creating," and

Mystery is found at the heart of all things. The universe no longer requires belief or unbelief, because the headlong rush of the stars, the struggle of life out of the sea and into the air, the growing awareness of a child, and the sheer creativity of it all are completely beyond belief. It is to these given facts that theology must now address itself, without the stopgap of "God." No one will listen if we try to smuggle the supernatural God in the back door.

This book is an attempt to develop a new theological language that is, in simplest terms, all verbs and no nouns. And since there are no nouns, there is no "God": all that remains is activity, the visible movement of a universe-in-process. This is the universe I describe as CREATING, INCARNATING, RE-CREATING—a PATTERNING of HAPPENINGS discovered in the moment of direct EX-PERIENCING. The reason for trying out such a language is an empirical one: the Hopi Indians of Arizona managed to talk almost exclusively in verbs, and apparently saw the world accordingly. The Hopi world was alive with movement, process, change. Nothing was static or permanent; therefore they had no Permanence called God. So, why not put Christian theology into a language structure like that of the Hopi? For there is nothing sacred about the noun—though we are forced to claim there is if we insist on keeping "God."

This experiment is meant to stimulate theological thinking in a new direction. Process theologies are appearing these days in great numbers, based mainly on the pioneering work of Alfred North Whitehead, Charles Hartshorne, and Teilhard de Chardin. But no one has tried to find a "process language" based on these insights. The present work makes an attempt. Not only have I tried to work out the premises on which such a language must be based; I have also tried to push the method as far as I am able. I find the method a persuasive one and I have tried to set it forth persuasively, not to be dogmatic but rather to present it with as much clarity as possible. I do not wish to defend this position to the death, as if I had discovered a once-for-all-time truth. For it is my belief that truth cannot be captured in words, but must be experienced. If the reader is already convinced of this position, there is no need to read farther. And, if the argument itself convinces him, there will be no need to turn to it again, for it will have served its purpose. He will be ready to live—indeed, will be living—what I call the theology of experience.

Since this book is aimed at the general reader as much as the academic, I have kept the notes to a bare minimum, using them simply to identify quoted material. The general reader will miss nothing by ignoring them; the scholar will, on the other hand, find material enough in them to pursue most of these matters in some depth. Biblical quotations are from the Revised Standard Version, unless identified as KJV (King James Version) or NEB (New English Bible).

It is always a hopeless task to trace the sources of one's ideas. The insights of teachers pass into the mind, merging with and restructuring what is there. Nevertheless, much of what is here grows out of the work of Northrop Frye, Norman Berrill, and Alan Watts, each of whose books have been a constant inspiration. Many of my insights are theirs and I must take the blame for whatever falls short of something better. Moreover, I would like to thank Mr. Watts for his personal encouragement at a time when this book was a messy, piecemeal first draft. In addition, I would like to thank Robert Gregg and Fred Bowers of the University of British Columbia, for many hours of discussion on my linguistic methodology. And finally, I would like to thank those who read the manuscript at various stages: Harold Epp, Keith Gilley, Tom Devine, and, of course, my wife, Shari, who patiently read it draft by draft, page by page, and told me when it just wouldn't do.

B. W.

Stanford, California

1

God's Death in Our Time

We are living in the first civilization in recorded history in which the proclamation of God has become a joke. In the aftermath of the "death of God" theology, a new way of treating the irrelevance of the old-style, supernatural God has become popular. Sometimes it too exploits the apparent absence of God—he becomes another draft dodger, or he has changed his name. But more often the wits and cartoonists simply utilize his all-too-human foibles as a springboard, creating endless one-liners that play on his extreme age, his Jewish son, his virgin mistress, and the tricks played on him by an enterprising devil. The recent movie *Bedazzled* manages to get a surprising amount of mileage out of this latter theme. To the pious believer such talk is blasphemy, stupidity, or pure nonsense—the irresponsible corruption of truth itself. But for the majority such remarks bring forth a belly laugh that is possible because there are so many of the pious left.

The most obvious features of modern life—gigantic business enterprise, scientific and technological advance, life in the pluralistic secular city, the war in Vietnam, the assault on space, the new morality—these concerns go on without recourse to any mention of God. Evangelists cry with prophetic rage against a godless world; theologians hail a liberating Christian atheism; sociologists register the demise of the supernatural; churchgoers hearken to the good old days with nostalgia; and college students, barely beyond their Sunday school religion, give a sigh of relief, able at last to breathe easier without the terrible burden of accounting for every action before the throne of God. And running through all of this is the increasing refusal to take the proclamation of the supernatural God with any seriousness at all.

Modern man has found that he can get along quite well without supernatural sanction or support. Yet, paradoxically, the churches are full, more and more are being built, and the President evokes the name of God often enough. But this is really only a facade—even among the most pious—hiding what Peter Berger calls the "secularization of *consciousness*"[1] and what Martin E. Marty has termed "the invisibility of unbelief."[2] For, increasingly, the Christian is becoming a victim of doublethink, much of it unrealized. He lives his life on pragmatic, humanistic, situational principles while claiming to live it on Christian ones. Moreover, he has to rationalize away his failures, such as his inability to make prayer a meaningful experience. If he manages to retain his faith, it is only by repressing the inconsistencies. Meanwhile, the world lures him on, for his friends, the "sinners" who are supposed to be so miserable, seem to lead a full life without the divine.

The confrontation between Christianity and the secular world view of modern man presents theology with a radical challenge. No superficial solution can be adequate—certainly not another explication of what the gospel "really means." Nor is it likely that a "translation" of the gospel into modern terms will solve the problem. Bultmann's "demythologized" Christianity and Tillich's method of "correlating" theological answers to existential questions provided a beginning but did not go far enough. For deep down, at the level of presuppositions, religion itself is out of step with our world.

This book attempts a new kind of solution based on a structural analysis of thought itself, and this analysis proceeds through language, the way in which *what* we believe, and *how* we believe it, grows out of our very grammar. And the theology here developed is founded on a new theological language which I believe is more in tune with the universe as we know it. But before we can develop this new language we must understand the old; we must see how the traditional theology of the past two thousand years has developed along the channels of our traditional grammar.

We like to think that every problem is distinctly modern. The decline of Christianity and the growth of unbelief, however, have been proceeding for at least six hundred years, along with a growing awareness that God is not needed to explain, justify, or govern the conduct of life. Centuries ago, church and state were integrally connected, giving God and religious belief the stamp of legality, and providing divine sanction for the laws of the state. With the gradual separation of the two came the realization that laws and governments were not divinely instituted but designed by men. The theory of the divine right of kings fell into disrepute. No longer bound by supernatural apron strings, government moved toward parliamentary procedures and soon developed the practice of rapid reform so common in our day. A similar development occurred in economics. In the Middle Ages, money was controlled largely by the church, which owned millions of acres of land throughout Europe. The development of trade and commerce in the sixteenth and seventeenth centuries soon brought the wealth into the hands of the mercantile class, where money changed hands according to the principle of supply and demand. Church strictures against, for example, the charging of interest were soon seen to be unrealistic. Reluctantly, the church gave way before secular change, but her loss of authority over secular life was never to be recovered.

The same relentless process occurred in every area of life. During the Enlightenment of the eighteenth century, philosophers such as Hume, Montesquieu, and Rousseau developed rational systems of behavior that did not require supernatural sanction for their authority but appealed directly to reason. During the American and French revolutions, freedom for man—as a *necessary* condition for human dignity—was emphasized with little stress on religious principles. Christian theology, which had formerly dictated ethical principles, was replaced by a secular emphasis on reason and logic. The development of Biblical studies in the nineteenth century quickly upset centuries of church authority by showing that Biblical documents were subject to human error, authorial prejudice, and editorial decision. The Word of God was challenged. In every area of human knowledge the pattern was repeated. The unknown, previously turned over to God or the supernatural, was gradually pushed back or given naturalistic explanation, effecting what Philip Leon has called an "intellectual, moral and spiritual saturation bombing."[3] There was no place left for God, who was gradually edged out of life.

The most important cause of the growth of unbelief, however, was the rise of science. Here the pressure on religion was the longest, most sustained, and most devastating. The history of modern science can be traced through a series of revolutions, each of which transformed man's understanding of himself and his universe. The first of these came with Copernicus in the sixteenth century. His

proposal of the heliocentric universe, in place of the much
older geocentric universe, shattered the cosmological
scheme of the New Testament, in which man had held the
central position. No longer was it possible to believe in
what Bishop Robinson has called the "three-decker universe,"[4] with earth in the middle, heaven above, and hell
below. Moreover, the orbits of the heavenly bodies, once
explained as the work of God, were soon explained in
terms of Newtonian mechanics. God, the creator and sus-
tainer of all things, soon became simply the creator, and
the maintenance of the universe was turned over to scientific principles. The inevitable result was the development
of deism in the eighteenth century, a last-ditch theory that
made God into the Supreme Mechanic who had wound
up the universe and sent it merrily ticking on its way. The
way was paved for Nietzsche's nineteenth-century cry
that "God is dead," Julian Huxley's comparison of God to
a "cosmic Cheshire Cat," and Altizer's cry that this dark
world is the dead body of God.[5]

The second scientific revolution affecting religious belief
was Charles Darwin's evolutionary theory, set forth in *On
the Origin of Species* (1859) and *The Descent of Man*
(1871). Bitter conflict arose between theologians and
evolutionists in the decades following the publication of
these books, and remnants of the conflict still survive. The
teaching of evolution in American schools is still a highly
controversial issue. From the beginning, evolution challenged the Christian view of man as a special creation
made "in the image of God" (Gen. 1:27), suggesting that
man was merely a highly developed "beast." The idea that
man had evolved from a long line of primeval worms,
rodents, and submonkeys was regarded as an insult to both
man and God. Moreover, it denigrated the supposed
"omniscience" of God, who could do all things, including

the miraculous creation of the universe in seven days. The much-popularized notion of the "survival of the fittest" turned creation into accidental progress, suggesting that man had "just happened." Moreover, because the initial stress was on physical evolution, the theory seemed to imply that man had no soul and was purely the result of blind chance operating on dead matter.

Evolutionary theory aroused considerable ire among theologians for at least one other reason. Agnostic and atheistic thinkers of the nineteenth century (the most outstanding being Thomas Henry Huxley, Darwin's "bulldog"), anxious to disprove religious superstitions, rushed to its defense, and claimed that evolution "proved" there was no God. Such ridiculous claims, of course, brought forth equally ridiculous responses from religionists: newly discovered prehistoric skulls of man, and man's own "vestigial" organs—fingernails, body hair, and tailbone, etc.—were said to have been "planted" by the devil as a snare for the unfaithful!

Ultimately, however, the effect of science on Christianity went much deeper than the simple development of new theories. Science developed a new methodology, which cut two ways. On the one hand, it replaced the rational method of the Greeks, who had assumed that nature worked on logical and reasonable principles that were discoverable by intellectual activity alone. On the other hand, it undercut the Hebraic-Christian reliance on truth as "the evidence of things not seen" (Heb. 11:1, KJV). The new method was that of observation, developed by such astronomers as Tycho Brahe, Kepler, and Galileo. For a time there was opposition, particularly when evidence was brought forward that contradicted ancient authorities. Galileo, for example, was criticized for claiming there were three moons around Jupiter, a claim that went against received opinion. His critics would not accept the evidence of looking through a telescope for themselves! But such opposition soon waned, and experimental science became the arbiter of truth itself. And today there is no escape. Science continually pushes back the frontiers of the unknown and technology turns the impossible into the everyday. In less than four centuries science has taken us all the way to the moon.

Science can be described in five ways, corresponding to its five main principles: it is empirical, quantitative, mechanical, progressive, and objective. These principles, however, have spilled over into nearly every other area of thinking, so that we approach all things "scientifically."

Science is limited to empirical reality, that is, whatever can be observed and measured. No theory is *scientific* unless it can be tested by experiment, observation, and measurement. This means, of course, that large areas of human experience are simply not available for scientific study. Moreover, science explains observable reality by mechanical principles that are reducible to mathematical equations and chemical formulas, thus limiting science to those aspects of the world that can be so reduced. And, finally, science is progressive, in the sense that it continually discards theories in favor of more comprehensive ones.

It was perhaps inevitable that these precisely limited principles would get out of control and master their masters. Pay careful attention to the empirical world long enough and you are wooed into thinking that the only important reality, perhaps the *only* reality, is what can be physically seen, tested, and measured. Continually work out your observations in mathematical and chemical formulas and you are soon hoodwinked into believing everything can be so worked out. Discard enough theories, refine enough equations, continually develop more comprehensive, progressive models with increased explanatory power (and more technological application) and you are soon hooked by the dream of perfecting human nature, economic structure, and political organization. Your science has turned into scientism, "which holds that empirical science is the sole source of genuine knowledge and that the scientific method is the only valid way to truth."[6] What you have is a new and idolatrous religion—scientolatry.

Any religion has its dogmas and mythology, and scientism is no exception. Taken dogmatically the quantitative principle of science becomes materialism, the insistence that reality is *entirely* concrete and measurable. Materialism reduces mental processes, emotional states, and spiritual experiences to the effects of colliding atoms and reacting chemicals. Taken dogmatically, the mechanical principle turns man into a mere cog in a huge cosmic machine. The result is a complete determinism in which he loses his freedom and powers of choice and becomes the pawn of determining forces—hereditary, historical, social, political, geographical, or economic. And, taken dogmatically, the progressive principle results in utopianism, the belief that science will eventually refine human nature, society, and government to produce a kind of Kingdom of Heaven on earth. This mythology of scientism has an insidious plausibility to it for the disillusioned proletariat that has lately lost its God, or revolted against him. With its claims of down-to-earth pragmatism and adherence to hard facts, this chest-thumping, nothing-but-ist view reduces man to an accidental aberration in the machine, a frustrated chemical dream whose salvation lies in bulldozing a stupid universe into servile obedience. And the fruits of this mythology are a host of materialist philosophies (agnosticism, atheism, existentialism), deterministic philosophies (Marxism, Freudianism, Skinnerism), and the relativistic viewpoints of the new morality and situation ethics. Every one of these positions—and they all have elements of truth—poses a challenge to traditional Christianity.

It is obvious, then, that science has shaken the Christian religion to its foundations, not only by challenging its views of man and the universe but also by substituting empiricism for faith as the ultimate criterion of truth. Science and scientism oppose Christianity, and all religions, by their refusal to accept, even on faith, what cannot be empirically verified. It seems clear that scientism has nothing of any validity to say about religion, since it is founded on illegitimate extension of the scientific method. But, in fact, science itself has nothing final to say about religious experience either, precisely because this experience is subjective and private, arising from what Martin Buber calls an I-Thou relationship with reality, whereas science is public and demands an I-It objectivity.[7] Once a scientist involves himself subjectively in his theory, he ceases to act "scientifically." But the realm of experience called "religious" demands precisely this kind of subjectivity, for it is verifiable only for the person who has had it.

Where then is the conflict?

If traditional theology (rather than just mysticism) had maintained the private, subjective nature of religious experience, it would have been immune to scientific attack. But theology has also maintained the truth of certain *historical events*—the seven-day creation of the world, the virgin birth of Jesus, the physical resurrection, the descent of the Holy Spirit at Pentecost—as necessary elements of belief. And it is precisely because such historical events enter the domain of objective fact that they become susceptible to scientific analysis and refutation. Protestantism has believed itself immune from this analysis because of its distinction between "profane history" and "salvation history," the latter of which is not amenable to scientific examination; and Bultmann has carried through with *Historie* (actual events in the past) and *Geschichte* (the meaning of these events in the here and now, in the life of the believer), "a legerdemain" which, notes Peter Berger, "loses much of its persuasiveness in any language but German."[8] But theology has continued to assert the real occurrence of these events, which are properly part of "salvation history." Theology has therefore forced the hand of science by insisting on miraculous events rather than stressing genuine, personal, inner religious experience, which is beyond the power of science to verify or refute.

According to this analysis, an awareness of what is really central to Christianity, personal religious experience, should be enough to resolve any conflict with science. By delineating the line between the domain of science (objective reality) and that of religion (subjective encounter), all grounds for conflict should disappear. But, in fact, it is not that simple. Such a solution works only for the Christian, who is able to defend his beliefs by the negative quality of their being impossible to refute. For the scientist this solution does not work at all, as J. S. Habgood has pointed out in his essay "The Uneasy Truce Between Science and Theology."[9] The problem centers on the Christian's claim that the content of his personal, religious experience is *objectively real.* In terms of the existence of God, the Christian claims that God exists because he has subjectively encountered him; and his statement of belief is logically unassailable as long as "exists" refers to something subjectively known. However, the Christian insists on taking one more step: he insists that the God encountered subjectively really exists, that God is a fact. And, in asserting the factual existence of God, the Christian places his religious beliefs squarely in the objective world of empirical science. The scientist who takes issue at this point is not overstepping his scientific method. He is, in fact, defending the integrity of his own factual knowledge, in which the unverifiable or unproved "fact" is always rejected and where no useless hypothesis or equation is tolerated. And, for the scientist, "God" *is* a superfluous "fact"—one which is (1) unverifiable and (2) unnecessary as a hypothesis to explain the universe.

This opposition becomes clearer when we consider the basic Christian claim that God made the world. Imagine a Christian and a scientist confronting the grandeur of a sunrise, the complex motions of a galaxy, or the symmetry of atoms in a DNA molecule. The Christian, looking at these with an eye for harmony and order, will call them, and the whole universe in which they are found, a creation. His conclusion will be the primary one of the Christian: this "creation" implies and necessitates a "Creator" who ordered and designed it. His statement "God made the world" is both an explanation for the world and a statement of faith. The scientist, however, confronting exactly the same data, will say what Laplace said when asked by Napoleon about the absence of God in his system: "I have no need of that hypothesis." Indeed, a scientist who rigidly follows his methodology must insist that it is impossible and unnecessary to construct a meaningful scientific theory of the world that includes a Creator. To include one would be a denial of scientific principles. Yet the conflict between Christian and scientist remains. They may well *claim* to understand each other's point of view but, in the end, will resort to their own "feelings" on the matter. The scientist will "feel" that the universe does not point to a Creator; the Christian will "feel" it does.

Thus the doctrine of God as held by most Christians—

God as a "fact"—is not a subjective belief that can be held alongside objective scientific facts; it is rather a rival of those facts. The doctrine of the existence of God, therefore, demands a decision, and an absolute one. Modern man must opt for science or religion, for the secular outlook or the sacred. He must either be a Christian believer —in which case the scientific rejection of God boils down to "sin" and "pride"—or else he must be a member of the scientific community—in which case he cannot believe in the Christian God without falling victim to doublethink. And which of these choices is really possible in the modern situation? It was therefore inevitable that so many people in our time would turn to secular atheism, openly endorsing life lived in *this* world, without God.

Gabriel Vahanian has called ours a "post-religious era."[10] The process of secularization, spurred on by the loss of church authority over secular life and the rise of science, has brought about a "post-religious temper."[11] Man has been gradually released from mythical world views; sacred symbols and transcendent beings have ceased to engage his attention; he has discovered that history is not in the hands of the gods but in human hands; and he has learned to look for the meaning of his existence in terms of *this* world, and *this* age (*saeculum*).

The Christian church has always tended to see the secular world as "outside the fold"—a world of doomed, pagan, sinful human beings. Augustine called it the *civitas terrena,* the "city of the earth," the destiny of which was to be everlasting banishment, torture, and hellfire.[12] The very structure of the church, as the bearer of the gospel, forces it into just such a position. If its message of salvation is to be taken seriously, the church must see the world as sinful and corrupt, thus setting itself in the role of judge and savior, continually applying the brakes in a world rumbling along in the wrong direction.

Totally apart from the truth or untruth of the gospel, it is apparent that the Christian view of the world is a highly dubious one. The secular city may need saving—it has ever since the Lord rained brimstone and fire on Sodom and Gomorrah, and Jonah was sent to preach at the wicked city of Nineveh. Judgment, condemnation, and verbal flogging may be appropriate, but in many ways the modern secular city is far from a state of total depravity. It has given us the new freedom of an age of leisure, the destruction of many ravaging diseases, personal emancipation through increased mobility, and an incredible extension of personal choice in many areas of life. Moreover, most of the creative giants of the last few centuries have been intensely secular in outlook and have worked out their productions within the city. Thus Christianity can hardly condemn the secular world while continuing to reap its creative and technological benefits. Christianity must face the fact that secularism is here to stay. As Harvey Cox has put it:

The effort to force secular and political movements of our time to be "religious" so that we can feel justified in clinging to *our* religion is, in the end, a losing battle. Secularization rolls on, and if we are to understand and communicate with our present age we must learn to love it in its unremitting secularity. . . . It will do no good to cling to our religious and metaphysical versions of Christianity in the hope that one day religion or metaphysics will once again be back. They are disappearing forever and that means we can now let go and immerse ourselves in the new world of the secular city.[13]

In 1944, Dietrich Bonhoeffer wrote these puzzling words: "We are proceeding towards a time of no religion at all: men as they are now simply cannot be religious any more. . . . How do we speak of God without religion . . . ? How do we speak . . . in secular fashion of God?"[14] Bonhoeffer's question defines the task. No longer able to oppose the secular world, Christianity will have to join it. Unable to talk of God in sacred terms, Christianity may have to learn how to speak of God in secular terms. Yet what this may mean, in short, is the end of God talk. Secular talk of God may not be God talk at all, for God is the central issue in the rise of secular unbelief. Albert Einstein once said that "in their struggle for the ethical good, teachers of religion must have the stature to give up the doctrine of a personal God."[15] The theological task in our day is a *Christianity without God,* and no matter how impossible this may seem—despite the apparent contradiction between "Christianity" and religion "without God"—we must face the possibility that there may be no other alternative.

But there is another reason, apart from the secularization of consciousness, that the supernatural God must go —an awareness among many Christian believers that something is profoundly wrong. The "death of God" theologians, most notably Thomas J. J. Altizer in *The Gospel of Christian Atheism,*[16] have brought us face to face with the impossible contradictions in the orthodox God of Christianity. The only way, they claim, to authentic Christian faith is through the atheism that denies this God. They assert that the only valid Christian faith today is, for many, the faith that takes over *post mortem Dei*— after the death of the supernatural God. Startling as this may be, sensational as their phraseology may appear, irreverent as their words may seem, these men must be heard, for Christian atheism speaks to more serious people in our day than the church would like to admit.

Like Laplace, who had no need of "that hypothesis," the atheistic theologians declare that modern man has no need of a God "in the gaps" of human knowledge. With advancing science, such a God is being "killed by inches, the death by a thousand qualifications."[17] He has no place in the modern scene because he is intellectually super-fluous. Moreover, modern man has no need of the religion that Karl Marx called "the opium of the people." Belief in God originating in the primitive fear of the unknown can only be "a prop or a sop."[18] Man must grow up and shake off dependence on God; he must shun the helpless groveling before the unknown that religion demands and sanctions. No longer can God be called in to win the war or save the System; if The Bomb goes off, man alone is responsible for his fate. Emotional cringing before the Celestial Manipulator can only be a mask for man's in-security or for the botch he has made of things. Throwing one's problems to God is little more than immature escap-ism, a devious method of not getting caught with the goods. The call to Christian atheism is, then, a call to bear the burden of responsibility, for the God that allows man to escape his responsibility needs to be abandoned as quickly as possible.

Above all, the "death of God" theologians take seriously the problem of evil. A God who "causes" or "allows" or "could prevent" the suffering of a child is morally in-tolerable. The omniscient God, knowing all things, can be held responsible for every misfortune that befalls us. No longer may we dismiss disaster with that glib phrase, "It is God's will." The answer to human misery and suf-fering is not God, for the God that allows human misery and suffering is not God at all, but Satan, and the God who allows Satan to live is his accomplice. Thus we come to the heart of the true atheism of our time—atheism that started with Blake and includes Feuerbach, Nietzsche, Camus, and Sartre—which insists that *God must die if man is to live*. Life under this morally intolerable God is life in the satanic mills under the reign of "an old grim-beard of a God,"[19] "the great blood-sucker,"[20] the "Hound of Heaven."[21]

Thus the "death of God" theologians move to a new and startling position. The situation of the modern Christian is, they say, like that of Estragon and Vladimir in Samuel Beckett's *Waiting for Godot*—without God, hoping there is a God, and waiting for him to appear. To be a Christian today demands more faith than ever before, for all the signs of God's presence are missing. There are no miracles anymore, and the mysteries of the world are set down in a phrase or a formula. Yet the Christian still waits, still hopes, still utters his midnight cry to the absent God. Christian belief in the God who is missing is a trust that someday he will no longer be absent, that one day he will come again into the midst of human life. Thus the "death of God" theologians point to faith that is *true* faith. When asked for a sign, Jesus refused to give it (with one exception), for a visible sign coerces man into unavoidable acceptance. The exception occurred when Jesus allowed doubting Thomas to feel his wounds, and Thomas had no choice but to acknowledge, "My Lord and my God!" (John 20:28). But note what Jesus said: "Have you believed because you have seen me? Blessed are those who have not seen and yet believe." (V. 29.) True faith demands that there be no signs—it is a free response before an utter unknown, the conviction of things not seen. Thus faith in a God who, according to all the signs, is "missing, presumed dead" requires more faith than would be necessary were there a single sign to point the way.

The dilemma of the modern Christian is complete. His religion is apparently founded on the existence of God, yet his religion must give up God to survive. William Hamilton has described this peculiar situation—that of being unable to reject the God who must be rejected:

> In one sense God seems to have withdrawn from the world and its sufferings, and this leads us to accuse him of either irrelevance or cruelty. But in another sense, he is experienced as a pressure and a wounding from which we would love to be free. For many of us who call ourselves Christians, therefore, believing in the time of the "death of God" means that he is there when we do not want him, in ways we do not want him, and he is not there when we do want him.[22]

With all sacred images smashed, with all the traditional arguments for God's existence refuted, and with God himself absent—the God who is intellectually superfluous, emotionally dispensable, and morally intolerable anyway—the secular Christian finds himself still dogged by the "Hound of Heaven." Rather than being able to take sides, rather than being definitely part of the "sacred" camp or part of the "secular," the Christian atheist finds himself with one foot in each. He is part of the "in" group and part of the "out" group—and unable to tell which is "in" and which "out." He is no longer satisfied with the traditional labels of "sacred" and "secular," for he has moved to a new position beyond belief or unbelief.

And here we have the key. As long as opinions are divided between "religion" and "science," all that can result are "religious" arguments why God must exist and "scientific" arguments why he must not—subjective knowledge that he is "real" and objective proof that he is not. As long as religion is in charge of the supernatural and science is in charge of the natural, all that can result are contradictory descriptions of the world with each side sharing half the truth—or less than half. As long as secular man thinks of God as a Mighty Being in a different realm, beyond contact, beyond investigation, and therefore unimportant—and as long as Christianity *supports* this view by retaining an inviolable "transcendent" realm where God is safe—religion and science will fail to resolve a conflict based on opposing sets of presuppositions.

The way out of this hopeless muddle appears when we see that both religious explanations and scientific explanations are abstracted from a *uni*verse that is whole. Despite the fact that science deals only with observable, measurable, mechanical, concrete reality, nevertheless, *in the very act of observing* this limited reality, the scientist is also examining Total Reality—including all that is invisible, immeasurable, and unexplainable. Interwoven with the warp of his physics and chemistry is the woof of mind and spirit. But it has been the peculiar habit of Western man to turn this interwoven fabric into a dualism of opposed "things": body and soul, matter and spirit, nature and supernature.

Now this habit is at once perceptual, conceptual, and linguistic. The human psyche is oriented primarily toward the visual sense. Seeing is believing. What is seen are "things," which are easily recorded in the nervous system as distinct images, with concrete qualities and clear edges. These images are carried over into the *imag*ination, which is primarily the use of the "inner eye" for rearranging images into new patterns. Language follows and reinforces this mental orientation toward images, for the primary kind of word in Western languages, the noun, is basically a sign for a "thing," or an "image" with concrete reality and distinct limits. A noun technically *de-fines,* that is, "sets limits to" or "marks off" what it names. Nouns therefore are the names of things that are marked off from their surroundings because they are *seen* and/or *imagined* as limited and separate. And, once de-fined, things no longer seem to be related to their surroundings. Thus the warp and woof of Total Reality—once they are designated as "matter" and "spirit," "body" and "soul," "nature" and "supernature"—become linguistically and imaginatively separate rather than integrally related. Imagining that only "matter," "body," and "nature" are real is like imagining a cloth made out of threads all running in the same direction; removing the warp or the woof inevitably means removing the whole fabric. Yet the history of Western philosophy is littered with just such absurdities—attempts to reduce the world to warp or woof. Religion and science are merely the most obvious examples.

The process of scientism is extremely easy to follow. Having linguistically and imaginatively separated "spirit" from "nature," the scientist then relegates the spiritual to a "supernatural" realm that is spatially *dis-tinct,* that is, "set apart." Finally, so much attention is concentrated on what is actually seen—concrete "matter"—that the world of "spirit" is "not known" through *ignor-ance.* And, if one is bothered by such nonempirical realities as "spirit," it is an easy matter to *ex-plain,* that is, "flatten out," "spirit," by reducing it to a form of "matter." (It is also possible, though less likely these days, to explain "matter" by reducing it to "spirit"—a tendency running through the various "idealistic" philosophies of Plato, Plotinus, Boethius, Berkeley, Kant, and Hegel.) These reductions are particularly common in Western thinking because, while our language sets up opposites, our philosophy abhors dualism, preferring the grandeur of a single comprehensive reality. Thus the philosophic scene is littered with many isms that reduce or ignore one or the other side of reality: materialism and mentalism, mechanism and vitalism, positivism and metaphysics, determinism and voluntarism, scientism and theism.

Any one of these philosophies presents a lifeless world entirely different from the dynamic, living, changing world of actual experience. The scientific materialist ends up with a dead world of intractable sludge, neatly categorized, pigeonholed, and shorn of all dynamic potential. The theist likewise ends up with an unchanging, immovable reality called God who—because he is absolutely infinite and eternal, omnipotent, omniscient, and omnipresent—is as unable to activate the world as a three-thousand-mile-high steel robot. The qualities of God, as set out by traditional theology, actually turn him into a huge static cripple, for the superultimacy of every quality removes the possibility of movement or change in any direction. The whole process of explaining—of breaking the world into factual chunks called "things" (nouns), "events" (verbs), and "qualities" (adjectives)—denies the unbroken fabric of the world we experience. Everything in our experience changes, yet our dualistic categories and linguistic storage slots are held in the mind as incapable of increase, modification, or change. The apparently innocent procedure of using words is, in fact, a devastating process of stripping reality of its life and movement and continual change. Nor has theology escaped the reductions of language, for theology has turned the reality behind religious experience into mere "facts" (actual events) by insisting that Christianity is a *historical* religion.

The death of God in our time now comes clear. "God" as an abstract "thing" in the supernatural realm above *is* dead because he is too abstract to be related to the world of the living. Yet, we sense "a pressure and a wounding," because we experience a Total Reality where God is still present, before he becomes "God." The absent God, the silent God, is only absent and silent because he has been linguistically crucified, killed by inches by a thousand qualifications. It would seem that God can be experienced but nothing can be said about him, at least not within the present system of linguistic description evolved by Western man. Thus the Hebrews were very wise in insisting that Yahweh should not be named.

Perhaps the most useful concept in this connection is Philip Leon's "descriptive philosophy."[23] Leon is primarily concerned about the effect of language which explains away reality, or reduces it. His criticism applies equally to science or theology, each of which has fragmented reality by the use of objective, factual language. What Leon advocates to counter this is "unprejudiced observation not aiming at anything more than description," rather than the usual kind of "explanation" that "precludes or annihilates." Descriptive philosophy, as Leon conceives it, "bids us neither 'believe that we may understand' nor 'doubt that we may understand,' but merely look that we may see."

> And if we make a habit of this patient and submissive waiting upon the revelation of experience instead of rushing in explanatorily where angels fear to tread, we shall find ourselves in an intriguing and exciting universe in which near and far, here and there, the same and the different, the one and the many, the quick and the dead, are antitheses useful, and indeed necessary, for a limited number of purposes, but not absolute, eschatological, like the separation into the sheep and the goats at the end of all things.[24]

It is, then, neither theology nor science that destroys,

but language itself. Yet this inevitably involves science, theology, and every human endeavor seeking to cope with reality through words. Moreover, language so shapes our thinking that most of our so-called common sense is founded on the logic of words. Benjamin Lee Whorf has pointed out that the basic concepts of Newtonian mechanics are natural extensions of the metaphysic of the Indo-European languages.[25] And, precisely because this metaphysic is inadequate for describing Total Reality, modern physics has had to abandon verbal language for higher mathematics. By a similar argument it can be shown that the basic concepts of theology are extensions of the same metaphysic. But, since this metaphysic is demonstrably inadequate for describing the wholeness of nature, is it not apparent that we need a new language—for science and theology? And by this we do not mean new words, but rather a different metaphysical foundation and a different grammar.

And, since the structure of Christian theology is an extension of grammar, the death of God in our time is merely one sign of the breakdown of a whole metaphysic. Man is struggling against linguistic chains rather than simply scientism or theism. God is no longer possible because the traditional concept of the transcendent is impossible, just as the concepts of substance and matter are impossible in a world of transaction and process—where matter turns out to be energy "mattering." Therefore, we propose a radical experiment—that of putting Christian theology into a different, non-Indo-European language structure that is demonstrably closer to the structure of the experienced universe. But first we must take a long and careful look at this structure with the intention to simply "observe and describe," trusting in experience alone to speak its imperishable truth.

2

The Seamless Robe of Nature

Let us, as Leon suggests, "make a habit of this patient and submissive waiting upon the revelation of experience," refusing to do more than "observe and describe"—accepting the fact that we can never *under-stand* nature, for nature is "standing under" us. But we can look and see, and that may be enough.

A mother cat will care for and protect her litter with the same dedication as a human mother. And her kittens, like children, will spend the hours in play, often pestering their mother until there is nothing left but immediate discipline. In her domestic concerns, nature brings forth a similar pattern in a thousand different ways. But while we may be comforted by our oneness with the world, we also suspect that we may not be quite "with it." Intelligence has lifted us above the security of ignorance. What is man among the stars? Our galaxy, a typical star cluster, contains more than 100,000 million flaming suns, and is but one galaxy amid an estimated ten billion. The light from the farthest of these galaxies has been speeding through space (at 186,000 miles a second) for two billion years, beginning its journey about the time the first protozoa were swimming in the first terrestrial seas. The length of this journey has given life on earth time to evolve an eye, a brain, and a telescope, so that we are now ready to interpret these distant rays as they arrive.

But what interpretation of this vastness can comfort us? Are we not lost in the darkness, like a candle struggling to light up a cathedral? Can our thoughts be more than chicken scratchings upon the surface of infinite mystery? These are the ultimate questions, which it is the business of religion to answer. Mankind has passed beyond the age of a tribal god, or even a global god, and many are beyond belief in any god. Yet the universe—with its vast array of spinning stars in a sea of space, with its marvels of emergent life and transcendent spirit—is *there*. We may be like the pebble that sets out to conquer the sea, but that is our challenge, and we must take it up.

We share this universe with stars we can never reach, but we make a mistake if we oppose ourselves to those stars. In the instant when the eye catches the image of a star, a vital connection is made that makes all the difference. The perceiving mind and the perceived star are incomprehensible apart from one another, and neither the external source of light nor the configuration of nervous energy in the brain is really a star. For a star is ultimately linked to the transformation of light, refraction, chemical change, and electrical impulse that occur in the process of *seeing*. In the moment of seeing, the material star and the mental star are bound together as tightly as a hand is bound to an arm. The real star, like the magnetic field of the earth, is somewhere between the poles.

Yet even the recognition that the reality of what we see lies in the seeing is only part of the story. The direction of seeing cannot be determined, for, in Dewey's term, it is "transactional."[1] The star becomes an image cast upon the mind and the mind becomes an understanding cast upon the star. As Teilhard de Chardin put it, "object and subject marry and mutually transform each other in the act of knowledge; and from now on man willy-nilly finds his own image stamped on all he looks at."[2] But lest this be regarded as a trick of words, it is worth considering just where man ends and his surroundings begin. The air he breathes is distributed to every living cell of his body, so that his skin becomes the merest membrane separating him from his environment. Indeed, in the act of breathing, man's "inside" and "outside" keep changing places. His body is full of water moving from the mountains to the sea, and carbon moving from the soil to the atmosphere. Man is so much a part of his surroundings that every movement he makes is equally a movement of the environment itself.

Most of the natural and social sciences are descriptions of man's connections with everything else. To say that character is formed by upbringing, attitudes are formed by social status and economic conditions, tooth hardness is a function of water content, and that general health is related to nutriments is to recognize the ecology of organism/environment on every level. Something of this attitude is apparent even in primitive astrology, where the life of the individual is "ecologically" tied to the pattern and movement of planets and stars. If we no longer believe in astrological relationships, nevertheless the fact remains that our bodies are made up of the same stuff as the stars —hydrogen, oxygen, nitrogen, carbon, and minute traces of a few more elements—and the proportion of these in the human body is related to the proportions in the stars. The story behind these building blocks of the universe is one of the most fascinating stories that can be told.

The elements found everywhere—in bone and brain, grass and mountain and sun—have been numbered according to weight from one to ninety-two, that is (in a

convenient shorthand), from hydrogen 1 to uranium 92.
Scientists have produced a dozen more unstable ones such
as americum 95, berkelium 97, and lawrencium 103, the
most unstable of which last for only a few millionths of a
second. We can simplify a complex and largely unmapped
structure if we say that these elements are constructed out
of three elementary particles known as protons, neutrons,
and electrons. Hydrogen 1, the simplest of the elements,
consists of one electron revolving around a nucleus of one
proton. To this basic structure, neutrons (neutral) may be
added, but the essential fact is that the proton (positive)
and the electron (negative) balance each other electrically,
making this close-knit unit possible.

The addition of one proton and one electron to this
hydrogen 1 atom magically changes it to another element,
helium 2, and the further addition of one electron and one
proton changes it to lithium 3—and so on, right up the
atomic scale. This principle of "addition" produces all the
marvelous range of elements from hydrogen 1 to lawrencium 103—including substances as different as oxygen 8,
chlorine 17, cobalt 27, tin 50, iodine 53, and the gold 79
that sparked centuries of searching for the fabled "philosopher's stone," as well as a rush into the wilderness of California and the Yukon. Yet what has been called the "addition" of particles masks a mystery, for something much
more complex is going on than the mere putting together
of pieces of stuff like blocks. Every element is totally new,
displaying unique qualities, and nothing in either the basic
particles or in hydrogen 1 provides a single clue about the
results of "adding" more particles.

These elements are scattered throughout the universe in
varying amounts, but the amounts are of profound signifi-
cance, for they tell a story of their own. Hydrogen 1 is
most abundant, making up the bulk of most stars, most of

the interstellar dust, and ultimately accounting for 55 percent of the total matter in the universe. Helium 2 accounts for 44 percent, and the other ninety elements account for the remaining 1 percent. Within this 1 percent there is a similar pattern of occurrence. The next three elements on the scale (lithium 3, beryllium 4, boron 5) are nearly absent; but then come carbon 6, nitrogen 7, oxygen 8, and neon 10—together making up nine tenths of everything that is not hydrogen 1 or helium 2. The remaining tenth contains all the other 83 elements, with an extra large amount of iron 26. Above iron, certain elements occur so sparsely that their value increases in proportion to their position in the series.

Now these relative amounts of the elements indicate the way in which they are formed. Scientists now believe there is a continual process of element-building going on in the universe, the evidence for which is overwhelming. The superabundance of hydrogen 1 suggests it as a basis for all the rest, and the tendency of the upper elements to break down, emitting radioactive particles, suggests that these are end products of a process that can go no farther. These upper elements appear to be too precariously built to maintain themselves, like a house of cards that is piled too high. And there is now the well-known fact of atomic fusion carried out in reactors—a terrifying process that belongs in the stars—the familiar symbol of which is the H-bomb. The H-bomb is really man's duplication of the first step of element building, the conversion of hydrogen 1 to helium 2, and the explosive and thermal power of this process is a clue about where the additional steps must take place: inside the stars.

There are several kinds of stars known to astronomers, but the majority fall into three main classes. Stars begin their lives as small, yellow dwarfs like our own sun. Burn-

ing with a heat of a few million degrees, these stars, known
as *main sequence* stars, are considered to be relatively
"cool" compared with the rest. Nevertheless, Sir James
Jeans once calculated that a pinhead of material from the
center of our sun would emit enough heat to kill a man at
a distance of one hundred miles. Main sequence stars
gradually evolve into middle-aged stars known as *red
giants*. In the process they become several hundred times
as hot and several million times as large, and give off a
soft red glow. Red giants gradually grow old and die, but
the actual death produces a third type known as a *supernova*, a fantastic display of cosmic fireworks set off by a
final explosion as bright as 100 million of our suns, which
scatters star dust across unimaginable reaches of space.

Astrophysicists believe that the elements are still being
created inside the stars, the biggest furnaces the universe
has to offer. Moreover, the evolution of a star, right up to
its final explosion into space, is intimately linked to that
process of element-building.[3]

Intergalactic and interstellar space is filled with raw
hydrogen. Given time enough, such cosmic dust forms
huge globules, brought together by the force of gravity,
and in time a star is born. As these hydrogen globules con-
dense, they become more closely packed and the internal
temperature begins to rise. At a temperature of twenty
million degrees, hydrogen 1 "burns" to form helium 2,
giving the star a helium core. This helium core slowly
grows, releasing immense heat to its outer layers, and
causing the star to swell into a red giant, a swelling that
accounts for about 99 percent of the star's lifetime. But
during this growth, at about 200 million degrees helium 2
starts to "burn" to form carbon 6, oxygen 8, neon 10, and
magnesium 12. These elements are produced for some

time (for the star has reached a temporary end point), which accounts for the high abundance of these four elements throughout the universe.

The temperature continues to rise, more rapidly now, and at one billion degrees minute quantities of oxygen 8 and neon 10 "burn" to form a whole new series: silicon 14, phosphorus 15, sulfur 16, chlorine 17, argon 18, and calcium 20. And, with a further doubling or tripling of the temperature, traces of this series convert to chromium 24, manganese 25, and iron 26. At this point, with fewer than one third of the elements produced, the red giant has exhausted its resources. Its end product, iron 26, is by far the most abundant element on the whole atomic scale above silicon 14, suggesting that red giant stars have been piling up iron 26 at this barrier for billions of years, like the terminal moraine of a glacier. Beyond this point, however, the fusion of the elements must go, for many elements have not appeared, including the crucial nitrogen 7, without which life as we know it could not exist. Yet nothing typifies the creativity of the universe more than nature's way past the iron 26 barrier.

A red giant, at the crucial iron 26 barrier, is an extremely unstable star, so that, as shrinking progresses and temperatures rise, a breaking point is reached. The central core of heavy elements suddenly "collapses" completely: the temperature soars to 100 billion degrees, and then the whole star blows up in an explosion visible for perhaps a million years. It becomes a supernova, visible in our own galaxy to the naked eye, hurling its dust into space at thousands of miles per second. In one stupendous event, a whole star, full of elements produced by a kind of stellar "cooking," is scattered through billions of miles of space in all directions, becoming a cloud of dust like the cloud from which it was born. But there is a difference, and a crucial one for everything to follow, for now the hydrogen is "contaminated" with minute traces of elements up to iron 26.

Again the process occurs. Another star is born, another cosmic fire is built. Time is no barrier, so that even with the unimaginable slowness of this process there is time for an endless number of such processes to occur. And it is going on before our eyes, in the hearts of all the stars. But a second stellar furnace works differently, for the hydrogen 1 now contains the contaminating elements, carbon 6, oxygen 8, and neon 10, from the beginning. New ingredients enter the oven and new paths are followed in the "cooking." Hydrogen 1 burns to helium 2 with a new process involving carbon 6, and changes occur right up the scale. The crucial missing nitrogen 7 appears, all the other missing ones up to iron appear, and the barrier at iron 26 is hurdled. And the subsequent supernova scatters every known element into the vast reaches of space. The contaminating elements from the first furnace have turned out to be the fertilizing catalysts in the second, and the minute traces of the elements now scattered through space are the stage props for the cosmic designing of life itself, including the mind of man, who contemplates its wonder.

In the past generation, evolution has become part of the mental furniture of the educated layman, who understands it as meaning not only that monkeys and men have a common ancestor but also that all terrestrial life has emerged from primeval sea life. But evolution must now be replaced by *cosmism*—the evolution of the whole universe—for evolution begins with the formation of the stars and the processing of star dust itself. Moreover, the evolution of the elements is going on today, as spectrum analysis shows, and supernova explosions are constantly occurring, scattering their creative enrichment through the galaxies. Thus, in the words of one astrophysicist, "The everyday objects with which we are familiar may be regarded as souvenirs of a stellar interior."[4]

Because all the elements are built from hydrogen, all their unique qualities are somehow implicit in hydrogen, as possibilities, just as the man is implicit in the child. Here is perhaps *the* "mystery of existence," strangely overlooked in a recent book of that title.[5] Nothing that chemists and physicists know about hydrogen and oxygen could lead them to predict the product of their combination—water. Nothing in the qualities of water could lead one to the designs of a snowflake or the pattern of winter frost. Nor could one predict that the addition of carbon to water could produce sugar, oil, gasoline, and the richest coffee cream. Thus, when the chemist combines chemicals to turn out a new product, he literally evolves it, for *e-volution* is the "turning outward" of matter so that what is *im-plicit* (en-folded) becomes *ex-plicit* (folded out); the hidden suddenly emerges.

What we can "observe and describe," then, are the continual changes of matter. Indeed, we can only stand in amazement before this awe-ful mystery, before the restless processes of element-building and development, inspired by a universe of infinite possibilities. Nothing more typifies this universe than the endless creating, evolving, building, changing out of which come all things.

The evolution of a star is but a part of the building of a whole galaxy. Billions of stars condensing out of hydrogen, like the condensation of steam into water droplets on a cool windowpane, produce a galaxy of stars; and all the features of a fully developed galaxy—the slow rotation, the localized star clusters within it, and the spinning of the individual stars—go back to the original turbulence of the contracting hydrogen gas from which the galaxy has condensed. Within the trailing galactic arms are found many specialized clusters: double and triple stars revolving around their own center as they are swept along in the larger system, and planetary systems revolving around a central parent "sun." And it is here, in a trailing galactic arm, on a tilted planet swinging round an average star, that man finds himself, peering out at the rest.

The planets provide a different kind of stage for a new kind of drama. A planet in a galaxy is as fragile as a seashell on a stony ocean shore. The parent sun must be stable and the surrounding space must be free of the explosive disturbance of the red giants. Here is found a quietude that is entirely different from the roaring stellar smelteries. Such a planet enjoys a steady warming glow, the temperature depending on the distance from its sun. Too close, like the planet Mercury, and its water sizzles away into space; too far away, like Jupiter or Saturn, and it remains in icy bondage colder than the poles of the earth. But if the temperature falls in the crucial range of liquid water, another kind of change is possible, for a whole multitude of the ninety-two elements are stable enough to combine in endless procession. Thus we come to a planet called Earth, where all is precisely right for the most to occur. The icy poles and scorching equatorial regions are moderated by the correct planetary tilt and spin, and the flow of tide and wind from these extreme regions produces comfortable temperate and mediterranean regions. In this ideal cosmic climate the most spectacular steps of change and development are possible, changes that lead to life itself.

The earth in its early days must have been, literally, unearthly, and scientists have put together a tentative description of what it was like. At first it was a huge globule of rotating star dust many times its present size, but gradually most of its hydrogen was driven into space by the pressure of sunlight, until it shrank to its present size. As contraction went on, heat built up inside, through the radioactive decay of uranium, thorium, and potassium. The center became a molten brew, with heavy elements sinking and lighter ones bubbling up in all directions. The whole interior bubbled and boiled, continually fracturing the upper crust with lava-like material thrust up from below. And along with this came water, squeezed out of the rocky crust of the earth like juice from an orange, until all the oceans of the world had bubbled into the atmosphere as steam. But slowly, as harder material collected at the surface in an ever-deepening layer, a plastic crust was formed that finally hardened into the igneous bedrock we know today. Four or five billion years have since passed, but lava still bubbles out of volcanoes, and earthquakes still remind us of a hardening crust unable to stand the pressure of its own shrinking and folding.

All the water of the present oceans shrouded the world in clouds—the earth was darker than a starless night. But finally the rains began, and they never ceased for thousands of centuries, for the water fell on burning rock and immediately sizzled back to the sky as steam. When finally the escape of heat to space allowed the water to remain, it inundated the whole land, speeding up the cooling and hardening of the rocky crust. The ceaseless beating of the rain on rising mountains dissolved the surface chemicals, ground the rocks to sand, leached out the salts, and carried it all down to the rising sea—and the ocean became the warehouse of the world's riches. Eventually, the rains cleared the sky and the sun shone through to her newest frontier for the first time in billions of years. It was a decisive step, for sunlight is needed to drive the chemistry of the sea onward to life.

The atmosphere of the primeval world[6]—as evidenced by our knowledge of chemistry, and by analysis of the atmospheres of the outer planets—was a mixture of poisonous gases: ammonia, carbon dioxide, and methane, bathed in a mist of water vapor. These ingredients together contain carbon, oxygen, nitrogen, and hydrogen—all of the essential elements found in living matter. But this atmosphere lacked one chemical that is present today, the ozone that mantles the entire earth in a thick layer miles above the surface, without which we would die in minutes from the deadly rays of the sun. But its absence in the beginning was essential, for it allowed the burning ultraviolet radiation to smash through the atmosphere, all the way to the surface of the sea.

Here we have the key to the dawn of life. Laboratory experiments have duplicated the ingredients of this early atmosphere, including the ultraviolet radiation. If ammonia and carbon dioxide are passed through a vacuum, exposed to an electric spark, and then bubbled through ordinary water, a number of important amino acids are formed. This experiment, easily performed in any high school classroom, duplicates the effect of ultraviolet radiation—or lightning—on the primitive atmosphere. No scientific demonstration could be more important, for amino acids are the basic ingredients of the proteins, which are in turn the warp and woof of all living things. What we see in the development of amino acids is a natural development of the primeval atmosphere, a progressive enrichment of the hot, steamy envelope of the earth by the action of sunlight.

Eventually, as the temperature of the atmosphere moderated, steam became hot water, and a warm organic soup was formed on the ocean surfaces. Here was the very womb of life. The popular notion of the origin of life in some sort of primordial ooze in an ancient swamp is unlikely in the light of the facts. It seems probable that the first living cells rounded themselves off from their surroundings in a warm, sunlit, mildly salty, tropical sea. Moreover, it must have occurred where warm water and fresh air and sunlight meet—on the surface of quiet ocean deeps, far from breaking waves and the turmoil of the shore's disrupting tidal flow. A million years—or a hundred million—is time enough for the slowest chemical building to occur, and time enough for the chemistry to build in every possible way, even along blind alleys that led to nothing more. But the building of acids went on, and, as some of them chained together into proteins, the surface waters became a colloidal solution of suspended protein particles. Thousands of other chemical developments proceeded too, but the vital chains of protein were there among the rest, a perfectly natural outgrowth of sea and air and sunlight and the stuff that was provided.

Like any complex chemical particles, molecules of protein are "sticky," that is, they attract passing molecules to themselves. Microscopic clusters of protein thus appeared, continually growing until they formed coacervates, collections of sticky particles enclosed in a watery "skin." This skin not only separated them from their environment but joined them to it, becoming a channel in and out for more molecules. The internal chemistry of a coacervate keeps changing, building up or breaking down according to external conditions. Molecules that do not "jive" with the rest are allowed to pass out, while those fitting the existing pattern are allowed to stay, and the cluster develops accordingly. The whole process sounds suspiciously like life itself, but it is not; it is a collection of inanimate chemicals displaying lifelike behavior. A coacervate reaching a high degree of chemical stability (building up as fast as it breaks down, rejecting some materials and attracting others) might be described as a form of prelife. Indeed, there is a continuity between lifelike chemicals and life itself, as Nobel Prize winner Wendell M. Stanley, of the University of California Virus Laboratory, once pointed out:

> It is difficult, if not impossible, to place a sharp line separating living from non-living things when one considers a series of structures of gradually increasing complexity such as . . . hydrogen, water, benzene, ergosterol, egg albumin, insulin, pepsin, tobacco mosaic virus, papilloma virus, vaccine virus, pleuropneumonia organism, bacteria. . . . Work on viruses has provided us with new reasons for considering that life as we know it . . . does not come into existence suddenly but is inherent in all matter.[7]

Life, from this point of view, is the natural outgrowth of chemicals growing and changing under the auspices of sunlight and sea, warmth and stillness and time.

A repeat performance of the dawn of life is prevented today by life itself. On the one hand, microscopic bacteria would devour the chemically rich coacervates almost as soon as they were formed. On the other hand, photosynthesis—the mysterious netting of solar energy by the living stuff of green plants—has prevented another beginning by releasing raw hydrogen, which combines with itself to form a shield of ozone in the upper atmosphere, thus screening out the ultraviolet radiation necessary for the creating of amino acids. At the same time, this ozone shield allowed the development of amphibious creatures that could leave the protective ocean to live and roam on land without immediate death from radiation. Some ultraviolet radiation leaks through—enough to kill an exposed worm within an hour—but surface life has long since learned to cope with it.

Living beings are chemicals in a state of stability, a dynamic equilibrium between too much growth and too much death. And for us it is precisely in those diseases in which this equilibrium is disturbed—in the runaway growth of a cell that becomes a tumor and then a cancer, or the living death of muscular distrophy—that our greatest terror lies. Yet the marvelous balance of life between these extremes was being learned when life was little more than a chemically rich sea. In one sense, the emergence of life was a miracle, considering the forces of heat and cold and sudden change to which we are still susceptible. On the other hand, life was inevitable, given enough time. Indeed, it was accomplished in a surprisingly short time, for the millions of years it took are as nothing beside the unimaginable slowness of a condensing galaxy or a building star. While life has evolved to self-consciousness, our own sun has progressed no farther than the "cooking" of hydrogen 1 to helium 2, and has at least six billion years ahead of it. The more we look at the slow march of chemistry, the more natural it seems: it has a rightness and a flow that draw us to its truth. Life is therefore no accident or freak but the expression of the universe itself, occurring wherever conditions are right. Thus, the existence of life throughout the endless galaxies is so much more than a mere possibility: how could it be otherwise?

Life is like the rainbow in the sun-shower, the sparkle on the sea, the whitecap on the wave: it takes so much to produce so little, yet the result is worth all the rest. Just so, the inhabitants of the universe give meaning to everything else in the universe.

Does it display too much pride to see man this way? Is

it not ridiculous to single out the particle of dust called man and find in him the meaning for the rest? Does not the grandeur of this marvelous creation lead inevitably to the idea of a Creator? On the contrary, the universe exists neither for God nor for man, but for itself—and man is a part of it. Every step up the evolutionary ladder gives meaning to what has gone before. The 1 percent of matter that comprises all the higher elements justifies the 99 percent that is only hydrogen and helium. A single flaming star gives meaning to the infinite blackness, and a tiny, fragile planet completes the largest sun. It takes a bed of coal to make a diamond, a whole mountain to make a peak, an ocean to produce a living cell, and a thousand species to make a man. This is the pyramidal structure of the universe: things of value rest on a huge foundation. It takes a whole human race to produce just one Plato, Beethoven, or Michelangelo. Could it be otherwise? Yet, is it not the Platos and Beethovens and Michelangelos who define the greatness of the rest of humanity? And is it not this human greatness which is the glory of a galaxy, or of a whole universe?

For many, there will be a lurking suspicion that the mind of man is somehow not a part of this. Can we account for the spirit of man by evolution? Can the mental evolve from the material? Is not the human spirit so far above the raw stuff of the material universe that we must account for it in some other way? Are we not forced into admitting that into the nostrils of man God *must* have breathed the "breath of life," after which "man became a living being" (Gen. 2:7)?

For many Christians, this is the Achilles' heel of evolutionary theory. But, for the scientist, such a God is merely a stopgap—something we plug in when explanation fails. The difficulty lies, of course, not in the theory but in our thinking, for we fragment reality into life and nonlife, matter and mind, and fail to see the continuity of all things. Moreover, seduced by material science, we have lost a sense of wonder about this so-called dead stuff called matter. And, thinking it dead, we need spirit to reanimate it for us. But if life emerges from matter, then life is somehow implicit in it, just as all the elements are implicit in hydrogen. And if we look carefully at evolution, we can see the slow unfurling of mind and spirit—not just in the flint chippings and cave paintings of early man, nor even in the bright eyes of cats and dogs. We can see mind and spirit appearing even before there were bright eyes and brains, and even before there was life.

The chemicals of life, even in their simplest prelife forms, show an uncanny responsiveness to light that reveals a dimension deeper than material appearances. All protoplasm, including the living cells of men and maples and microbes, is irritable—that is, responsive to what goes on outside itself. It is light-responsive without eyes, nervous without nerves, contractile without muscle tissue of any kind. What we call awareness is present in life from the beginning, in the protoplasm of which life is made. Infinitely attenuated it is, but present nonetheless. Responsiveness to light, irritability, and general sensitivity lead to specialized cells of different kinds, and these in turn lead to nervous organs for more refined awareness. These organs, through the increasing complexity of impulse, develop nervous connections and gradually evolve into specialized centers of sensitivity—eyes and ears and taste buds. Refinements appear, more stimuli enter the system, and a central switchboard develops to organize the impulses. And this switchboard, already manifest in primeval sea worms and starfish, is the beginning of a brain. Sensitivity becomes perception, irritability becomes awareness, and the imprints of experience on the cells of the organism are the beginning of learning. Every subsequent development is therefore implicit from the beginning in protoplasm. Awareness in living things becomes self-awareness in man and, later, the self-transcendence experienced by poets and mystics and ordinary man in his everyday dreams. But the amazing feature of the whole process is the absence of any indication of what may appear at the next stage of growth. But the most wondrous fact of all is that everything, all of life and man himself, is somehow implicit in the elements of the universe, which in turn are implicit in the basic stuff of everything, hydrogen. To deny the miracle of the emergent human spirit one must deny a thousand similar miracles, including the miracle of star dust itself.

Yet we need not look to the stars to confront the miracle. We are made out of the bread and milk and meat and fruit that have grown out of the dust of the earth— "dead" matter! Life exists because the possibility for life is present in the soil and water of the ground on which we walk. Man is built out of matter forged in the stars, dust on the surface of a planet arranged into living form, and carries the whole history of the universe along within himself. Ultimately, he is a harmony of hydrogen, a dance and pattern that has been building up note by note, chord by chord, through endless time. Yet he is not only a pattern of matter in the universe; he is also a design that reflects what the universe has done, and who finally contains an image of the universe in his own mind. He is, in fact, so much a part of all the rest that he might well be considered a symbol for the cosmos, a point in the total design where everything the universe has ever done comes together and thinks about itself, marvels at itself, tries to understand itself, and sorrows over itself. In Hamlet's words, "What a piece of work is a man!"

For hundreds of years Western man has considered himself a distinct and separate being, apart from nature, totally disconnected from other "things," as tables and chairs are disconnected from each other. Moreover, philosophical analyses of reality have often been built on analyses of such disconnected "things"—Plato's "bed" in the tenth book of *The Republic* and Descartes's "lump of wax" in *The Meditations* being perhaps the most obvious examples. But not only is the view of human beings as "things" a fallacious one; it is now becoming apparent that the whole separation of "things" from one another conceals the vast unity of everything. The idea of the isolation of things, as Teilhard de Chardin points out, is "an intellectual dodge":

> Considered in its physical, concrete reality, the stuff of the universe cannot divide itself but, as a kind of gigantic 'atom', it forms in its totality . . . the only real indivisible. . . . The cosmos in which man finds himself caught up constitutes, by reason of the unimpeachable wholeness of its whole, a *system,* a *totum,* and a *quantum:* . . . all three within a boundless contour. . . . It is impossible to cut into this network, to isolate a portion without it becoming frayed and unravelled at all its edges.[8]

The universe is an undivided whole, a seamless robe; nature, including human nature, is not a heap of fragments but a unified field of interrelationships in which nothing can be considered apart from anything else. The unity of all things is with us always, even if it continues to remain just behind, below, or beyond the limits of our perception.

All things by immortal power
Near and far
Hiddenly
To each other linked are,
That thou canst not stir a flower
Without troubling of a star.
                    —*Francis Thompson,*
                    "The Mistress of
                    Vision," Canto XXII.

The universe is not a creation, in the sense of something completed and final, but rather a continual process of creating and evolving. The isolation of things as if they were static and permanent is a useful procedure for analysis but is ultimately untrue to the facts. What we call things turn out to be, in the long view, processes—though we cannot, perhaps, be blamed for the mistake. We gaze at the sky, at constellations unchanged since first charted by Babylonian astronomers, and unwittingly think that the stars last forever. Yet even the stars grow and develop and die, leaving an enrichment behind. Speed up the camera a million times and the mountains rise, fall, and erode like drifting snow; speed it up a few million more times and the stars swell and burst like children's balloons. Everything turns out to be a dynamic process of change—a kind of magic, we might say.

The same is true of human bodies and minds. We grow out of the sea and soil, and our blood streams flow with the saltiness of the primeval oceans from which we came. "All is change," said the Greek philosopher Heraclitus. "Only change is changeless." Man is not explainable as a being, for he is an eddy of star dust, a constant becoming. Cells in his body are born and die every second, for change is the essence of life, and when change stops death is upon us. Life and mind are growth, and growth is *de-velopment,* the continual "un-folding" of new possibilities. The universe is creating the new, the different, the marvelous, even as we watch. How can we miss it? It is there, in the growing of an acorn into a mighty oak, the blooming of a flower from a bud, the blazing up of a sun out of the dust of space. Creation is what we see in every moment—in the continual building up and breaking down of galaxies and mountains, trees and animals and men, laughter and love and human hopes and human fears.

No matter where man turns in the universe, he encounters the same seamless robe, and no matter what thread he pulls, he finds he is in turn pulled from somewhere else. Every new reach into the unknown brings forth a marvel that shatters the old vision. There is no way to study this world from above, for man is inside it, a part of the unknown for which he reaches, and the marvels he finds are partly those of the reach itself. Yet, if man wants it any other way—if he wants to "fix" the world in a formula, to nail down all the loose edges, to create his own static little world—then the price to be paid is the death of his own spirit. Freezing the universe means freezing oneself along with it, but probing its mysteries turns out to be, paradoxically, probing the innermost depths of one's own being.

Have we explained anything? Not at all. The creation of all things out of hydrogen can be described, but never explained, for it would somehow involve explaining the explainer. The most that science can do is provide ever more exact descriptions of what takes place and what took place. The final mystery of existence, the great *why,* is hidden, utterly beyond the power of thought, vision, or language.

But, somehow, describing it is enough. The evolving universe is now universally accepted by scientists and edu-

cated laymen, even while it fails to bring man any closer
to that *why*. Moreover, a fully scientific description of the
universe reveals that nothing is without mystery. The old
kind of miracle, the so-called supernatural event, is now
seen to be inadequate and unnecessary in a universe whose
every particle is another mystery. Modern man will accept
this vision, not because it explains things and not because
it gives him ultimate security but because it unveils the
awesome grandeur of the world he knows.

If modern man refuses to talk of a transcendent God, it
is because that kind of talk turns mystery into words and
wonder into credulity. He will not accept any reality beyond this world, for this world holds so much, and almost
nothing is really known. The stars come and go, leaves
bud and fall, man is born and dies—and we can only "observe and describe" in utter amazement.

Where can theology go from here? It has but two
courses. On the one hand, theologians can maintain their
admittedly inviolable position, asserting the reality of the
transcendent God—in which case theology will die a pain-
ful and protracted death. Inviolability means nothing, for,
as J. S. Habgood has said, "theology, while remaining
logically unassailable, has ceased to matter."[9] On the other
hand, theologians can face up to the absolute dilemma of
this first course and seek to escape it, by learning to speak
in secular fashion of God. The time has come for theologians to admit that they must choose this second way. To
try to preserve the old-style theology alongside the scientific vision of reality is to be guilty of doublethink. The
decision is an absolute one. The fences are down, which
means that compromise is impossible, since there is no
place to sit somewhere between.

What modern man wants in theology—*if he wants theology at all*—is a radically different approach that will syn-

thesize two incompatible pictures of the world without
forcing him to abandon one of them. And it should be
clear by now that what will emerge, what *must* emerge, is
utterly unlike anything Christianity has so far known.
Theologians must virtually begin all over again, assuming
that everything theology has so far said *may* be subject to
error. Yet theologians must begin not with a review of
what has gone before, or even with the language they have
so far used, but with the fundamental assumptions that lie
at the basis of language and thought. This means that the
very nature of human thinking must be examined, for it is
there, in the depths of the human mind, that the problem
begins.

3
Origins in Antiquity

It seems to be true that people are not persuaded by logical argument so much as by their willingness to be persuaded. Theologians meeting to discuss differing points of view—Roman Catholic or Protestant, fundamental or radical, theistic or atheistic—have a built-in thickheadedness against the opponents' arguments. This fact is the bane of sensible discussion in nearly every area of life: between labor and management, new left and establishment, Kremlin and Pentagon, old and young.

The problem often resides in the fact that opposing points of view are usually argued at a surface level, with no real penetration to fundamental issues, as if one could make oil paint compatible with water paint simply by changing the colors. The real sources of difference are often those deeper fundamental assumptions which make up what R. M. Hare has called a *blik*—a predisposition to see the world from one's own habitual point of view.[1] The actual position that a person explicitly defends is not the place to attack, any more than one would attack an army at its strongest point. On the contrary, the place to begin, as Whitehead suggested,[2] is with fundamental assumptions. Whole civilizations and cultures adhere to certain habitual *bliks* that appear so obvious that they are completely unrecognized. People within a culture simply know of no other way of dealing with things, and it is here that the real source of difference lies. If Whitehead is correct, opposing philosophies *within a single culture* unconsciously may hold similar assumptions about the world.

Now, if basic assumptions are the proper starting point, it is not entirely clear how one is to begin. The logic at the basis of thought is curiously hidden from view. The apparent ease with which we think up ideas masks a vast maze of unknowns. Thinking, in this respect, is like walking or looking: no one knows how he uses over six hundred muscles to place one foot in front of another, or how he uses the eye to transfer the outer world inside. Physics and chemistry tell us nothing about these things. In the same way, the basis of our thinking is deviously hidden. We lack the conceptual tools to examine our assumptions, because every tool we can devise involves the same set of assumptions. Probing thought by thinking results in a vicious circle.

It is impossible to justify one's own qualifications for an examination of basic assumptions. For such an examination implies that one has risen above them, or is somehow free of their determining power during the examination. There is, in fact, no way to prove logically that basic assumptions determine man's thinking, for any deterministic theory implicates the theorizer and the theory itself. Like Plato's people facing the wall of the cave, we have no way of knowing the sunlight exists. If man is in chains there is no man free enough to discover it. It is therefore impossible to put forth more than a tentative theory of basic assumptions, recognizing that these assumptions blind some men more than others, and no man absolutely.

If we look closely at the conflict between science and Christianity, a number of interesting assumptions emerge.

Christianity insists that a transcendent realm is necessary; science insists that it is not. At first glance these seem to be two different assumptions. But, in fact, both views are founded on a deeper assumption: that the "transcendent" realm under discussion is a realm *separate from* the natural world. In short, the existence of God is debated within the single basic assumption that God—if he exists at all—exists separate from that reality called nature.

Another basic assumption is revealed in the *objective* principle of empirical science. Although science goes back to the time of the ancient Greeks, empirical science did not emerge until the sixteenth century. One of the reasons for this is the fact that the Greeks had not fully separated themselves from nature. For them, the gods and nature and man were subject to a higher principle, the logos, and they believed that this principle was discoverable by reason. Greek science was therefore *deductive;* the notion of performing an experiment to test their deductions never occurred to the Greeks. By the sixteenth century the humanistic movement had so altered human thinking that men began to see themselves in quite new ways. Man was seen as above nature—that is, separate from it. This emancipation of man from his world effected an *objective* attitude toward reality, an attitude that gave rise to experimentation, observation, and *inductive* science. The appeal to truth was no longer to authorities like Aristotle but to nature itself. At this point science did not conflict with Christianity, for the Bible taught that man was created higher than the beasts. Moreover, God was not subject to a higher logos: he *was* the Logos, and his ways were discoverable only by actual observation. Human reason could not penetrate God's plan; the book of nature had to be read, just as did the book of Scripture. It is apparent, then, that the Christian view of man and the scientific view, no matter how different they appear at first glance, both share the basic assumption that man is a being *separate from* nature.

These two basic assumptions reveal that science and Christianity, now rivals, emerged from a common understanding of the universe and a shared assumption that man, God, and nature are separate aspects of a total reality. But it is apparent that such an understanding is by no means universal. The Greek view of man as a part of nature is akin to many non-Western and primitive world views; and the Hebrew view of man as separate from nature and God must have arisen from an earlier view in which the distinctions were somewhat blurred. As Robert Redfield puts it, "if later world views might be compared with reference to a triangle of these three conceptions—Man, Nature, God —the primary world view was one in which the triangle itself was not very apparent."[3] The Hebrew view, which is basic to science, was a unique achievement in the history of human thought, but one which has gradually come to dominate as European nations gained supremacy throughout the world.

The modern disaffection with religion, as noted earlier, centers on talk of a "transcendent" God. The end of God talk, however, can mean at least two things. On the one hand, it may mean pure atheism: while *assuming* that God and the universe are separate, one can deny that this separate God exists. This is the position of science and its related philosophies, which ground themselves in empirical principles, and it is a position that is bolstered by theology when it insists on the "otherness" of God, when "otherness" means "separateness." Thus atheism has been caused, at least in part, by the failure of theology to emphasize the "nearness" of God—the doctrine of the Holy Spirit.

On the other hand, the end of God talk and the death of God can mean the refusal to separate the secular from the sacred, with the insistence that we learn "to speak in secular fashion of God." In effect this means a new theological language based on new presuppositions; it means that our description of the seamless robe of nature somehow *includes* a description of God, though our divided way of thinking hides it from us. If theology is to survive at all, it must respond to this modern denial of the transcendent God: it must find a way to make the "divine" meaningful for our time; and it must find the language that can accomplish this task. And the key may rest in precisely those non-Western and primitive views of the world as a unified interpenetration of God, man, and nature. For it is apparent that the fragmented universe of modern man is a unique achievement, which poses a fascinating historical question: Where did it come from?

Precivilized man lived immersed in a kind of magical forest. The hills and streams, sky and stars, were alive, animated by spiritual forces largely indifferent toward the affairs of men. Primitive religion consisted of an elaborate system of rites and formulas designed to "scientifically" control these forces, and religious specialists varied from beneficial medicine men who healed the sick to witch doctors who used their terrible magic to channel the forces of the universe against their enemies. The animating force of "spirit" had not yet been streamed off into another realm "above" or "beyond" the dead world of material stuff. Mountains and trees were the living brothers of men, and human clans and moieties responded to nature in I-Thou involvement, relating themselves to specific animal or vegetable species, which were therefore considered sacred. The tribal structure thus extended out into nature, taking in the whole universe, and cosmic events had a profound effect on humanity. This inclusive cosmological vision was, in one form or another, the primary world view of virtually all uncivilized or precivilized peoples, including the ancestors of the Hebrews: the Sumerians, Egyptians, and Babylonians.

Modern man is coming back to the inclusive cosmological vision, but with a difference. Ecological studies are finding that man's life is intertwined with the movements of the sun and moon, migrations of animals, and the advance and retreat of polar icecaps. Evolutionary theory is finding that man's roots go back to early primates, backboned fishes, primeval sea worms, and the element-building stars. And biological studies reveal that life extends to an attenuated prelife hidden in the heart of inanimate matter. The primary world view, full of quaint beliefs about man's relation to the world, turns out to be surprisingly close to the societal, organismic, transactional models suggested by advanced science. It would seem that, having developed a fragmented, isolationist model of reality, we are now having to return to certain fundamental ways of seeing ourselves that stretch back to the dawn of human thinking.

And yet, the divided world in which man, God, and nature are distinct is absolutely *fundamental* to Christian theology. Underlying Christianity is a basic metaphysical-cosmological dualism of "heaven" and "earth." Every theological doctrine seeks to explain or assert a *relationship* between God and the world. The Creation doctrine establishes that God is prior to, superior to, and responsible for the universe. The doctrine of the Fall asserts that man's sin has brought about a disjunction, a breaking of communication such that the metaphysical distance between these two realms has increased. The doctrine of the incarnation asserts that God has reestablished communication between heaven and earth, and the redemption of man is a metaphysical decrease in the distance between these two realms. Finally, the doctrine of at-*one*-ment, which refers to man *and* his world, asserts a final change in the relationship, such that the distance between heaven and earth completely disappears. The final vision of the Apocalypse is that of a garden at the center of a city that has been exalted to heaven, so that all the creatures of the earth surround God in a final harmony. Apart from the truth of either the divided universe or theological doctrine itself, it is clear that traditional theology depends completely on these divisions. What would happen to theology if these divisions proved to be ultimately unreal?

The key question is how the primary world view of precivilized man evolved into the Hebrew world view— how the unified cosmos became divided. This question penetrates to the roots of human thinking, to the level of those elusive fundamental assumptions, and it challenges the powers of historical reconstruction to the limit. Moreover, there is no way to get at fundamental assumptions other than by examining their expression in numerous facets of life—language, social structure, economics, and politics. Thus it is impossible to provide more than tentative suggestions, many of which may well be sheer guesswork.

Since primitive man did not make very definite distinctions between himself, nature, and God, his total perception of reality *must* have been entirely different from that of modern man. What this means is difficult to grasp, but studies of nonliterate and literate Africans illustrate some of the differences that may apply to primitive man.[4] In a nonliterate society the whole educational process leads the individual to see himself as part of a much larger unit, the family or clan, rather than as a self-reliant, independent being. Since individual ambition and initiative in such a culture has little cash value, the individual has no opportunity or motive for integrating himself along personal lines. Each man identifies his ambitions, goals, and concerns with those of the whole group. At the same time, while intellectually subordinate to the group, the individual develops great freedom and expressiveness at the temperamental level. Feeling and emotion are the primary modes of existence for nonliterate man, whereas literate man moves in the realm of ideas. Intellect depends upon clarity, objectivity, coolheadedness, whereas emotion tends to engulf a person in an overwhelming wave of subjective involvement. This involvement is the hallmark of the primitive world view.

Marshall McLuhan has pointed to the vast differences between the visual world of modern man and the auditory-oral world of preliterate man.[5] The Western child is introduced at an early age to light switches, uniformly shaped objects, and appliances, which constrain him to think in a highly visual manner, with an acute awareness of temporal relations and simple, mechanical causation. He becomes accustomed to the uniform, repeatable, predictable world of city life—a spatially organized world of multistoried buildings, uniform city blocks, evenly spaced lampposts, and push-button gadgetry—a world that is organized visually. The child in preliterate cultures, however, grows up in an educational environment centered on the spoken word—on oral instruction, ritual stories, magical stories, and the ever-present sounds of the magical forest. He is taught to listen—indeed, not to listen can mean instant death—whereas the Western child must learn to blot out most of the background noise of machinery and traffic if he is to survive at all. Primitive religion centers on words, incantations, and verbal formulas whose magical operation depends on exact repetition. Moreover, individuals are *named* after certain desirable qualities and, in addition, often have secret names to protect them from the deadly verbal magic of the black magician.

These differences structure the whole psychology along widely different lines. Modern, visually oriented man is man directing his attention to one thing at a time, concentrating on a single task, organizing his days by a linear calendar, noticing things by separating them from their surroundings. Primitive, oral-auditory man is man enveloped by sound with its characteristic blurring of distinctions and its insistent call to the hearer. One cannot "listen away" as one can look away. Sound is more pervasive than sight; it emerges from the whole environment, and any confusion about its real origin creates an immediate sensation of mystery. Sound has an immediacy, a once-for-all-ness, that is commanding, and a dynamic quality that elicits response and involvement. The sensory world of primitive man, therefore, leads him to perceive the world as a gestalt, an organic, relational whole, as against the fragmented, linear-sequential world of visually oriented modern man.

All of this might well be pure speculation if it were not documented. However, educational research on nonliterate Africans has uncovered evidence for the principal psychological differences described.[6] Nonliterate Africans apparently cannot grasp a story or learn factual material from Western films, even when presented in their own language with ultrasimplified plot lines. Moreover, none of the everyday objects that appear on the screen can be remembered, or even distinguished from the background. Nothing, therefore, can be taught to the nonliterate through movies. The reasons come down to basic perceptual differences. The perception of three-dimensional Euclidean space from a two-dimensional movie screen depends upon a visual detachment that literate man has developed through reading. This detached use of the eye catches a whole picture by focusing the eye somewhere just in front of the picture so that all the parts of the screen and the spatial relationships between the objects are immediately grasped. This visual detachment actually allows literate man to perceive depth in two-dimensional pictures. Moreover, it is a skill quickly mastered by the nonliterate as he learns to read. (This conjunction of three-dimensional perception and literacy accounts for the sudden development of perspective in the paintings of Brunelleschi and Masaccio in Florence, and the Van Eyck brothers in Flanders, at the beginning of the fifteenth century during the full tide of the literary Renaissance.) The nonliterate African, however, becomes involved, empathetically "with" what he sees, and uses his eyes as a visual feeler, roaming over the objects on the screen in random exploration. Consequently, he fails to grasp the spatial relationships and important distinctions between things on the screen. One could say he has not yet developed I-It perception.

What we have been describing is the differences of perception between preliterate and literate man. A great transformation, perhaps the most profound psychological development in human history, would seem to have occurred somewhere between primitive, tribal, nomadic life in the forest and modern, political, settled life in the urban setting. What were the factors that changed the perception of reality, and therefore the whole world view, resulting in the fragmented, isolationist world of Hebraic and, ultimately, scientific man?

The primary factor, as the above analysis suggests, was a change in environment. Nomadic man lived in forest and cave with relatively undeveloped community life and very few possessions. Around ten thousand years ago, urban

life began, and within four thousand years man had discovered or invented most of the techniques at the basis of
civilization: agriculture, the selection of fruits and cereals
and livestock, the skills of pottery-making, cloth-weaving,
and metallurgy, the beginnings of political structure, and
the all-important specialization of function. Within the
first urban settlements, amid these socioeconomic developments and specialized activity, rational thought as we know
it began to emerge, laying a foundation for all that was to
follow.

The new environment of the man-made village slowly
developed a new perception of the world. No longer
directly dependent on natural sources of food, urban man
grew his own. Hunting was relegated to a few, so that the
majority saw meat from the kill out of its natural context.
The slow extrication of man from total submergence in
nature had begun, laying the foundation for the modern
fallacy that man can get along without nature altogether.
Alongside these changes in the relation to nature, urban
man was building a society based on human specialization.
As tool-making and canoe-digging became "trades" carried on by individuals, rather than tribal projects, each man
became less *obviously* reliant on the group. His occupation
made his livelihood a personal matter, and he began to see
himself as a separate, unique being. The ground was laid
for what L. L. Whyte has called "the primary duality":

> Nature everywhere has the same general form, but
> dual aspects arise as soon as distinctions are made.
> The primary duality from which all others spring is
> the separation of this system here and the rest of
> nature, of this particular process and its whole en-
> vironment. There is nothing incompatible about this
> duality, which is inherent in any world which can be
> conceived. But from it arise all the harsh intellectual

dualisms which separate what is not separated in nature.[7]

Given time enough to think, man eventually discovered his own thinking. He became aware of himself as a persisting subject, separate from the changing events of nature, and a basic subject-object dualism became the primary structuring device in his thought and expression. It was therefore no accident that the primary convention of all the Indo-European languages—and it was among Indo-Europeans that most of these urban developments occurred—became the convention of subject and object.

Nomadic man had few possessions—a few weapons and the clothes on his back—and these had the same matter-of-factness that our own belongings have for us. But the rest of nature was invested with magical properties, which meant that his whole universe was mysterious. The development of urban life, however, began the mania that has never ceased—the accumulation of more and more personal possessions. These increasing products of human effort gradually replaced the magical forest with an artificially constructed environment, thus creating a barrier between man and nature. Man's environment became desacralized in the sense that his surroundings became a protective, self-designed, urban settlement rather than the raw forest. And the desacralization still continues, as the man-made environment of supermarkets, suburbs, cars, and cloverleaves increases, gradually Los-Angelesizing the whole countryside.

Along with the physical separation from nature, the desacralization of physical environment, and increasing individualization, proceeded the equally revolutionary changes wrought by the development of language and writing. These social skills can be considered within the broader context of evolution itself—a phase that Teilhard de Chardin calls "the deployment of the noosphere"[8]—for they involved among other things the entrenchment of all these cultural developments in the very structure of language and thought, and, therefore, in the perceptual and conceptual apparatus of the nervous system itself.

Nature is continually changing, developing, growing. Movement and process are inherent in wind and wave and life itself. Even human experience is brought about by change—the onset of an event, the transmission of light and sound waves to the eye and ear, the generation of nervous impulse and mental pattern. Where nothing changes, nothing happens, nothing is seen, experienced, or known. Yet how is all this to be captured in words? How can we net the things that refuse to stay still, that insist on wiggling out of control? Above all, how is one to remember a world that is never the same twice, where leaves fall and bud again, and the clouds are ever new?

Memory, the organized record of experience, naturally retains the clearest images from stable or repeated situations, such as the primary shape of mountains, or the final shape of a mature leaf in midsummer. The erosion of mountains is unseen, and the movement of waves can be subordinated to the stable qualities of constant shape and behavior. Images—the basis of imagination and language —capture these stable qualities. The essence of an event can be crystallized into a stable image, so that the processive operation of nature is reduced in the mind to static glimpses abstracted from the total process. The mind, in the very act of grasping at nature, reduces and simplifies. As Whyte points out, "that special part of nature which we call thought thus became alien in form to the rest of nature; there grew up a disjunction between the organization of thought and the organization of nature."[9]

Simultaneously with the development of memory, the retention of images, and the crystallization of experience came the genesis of language. As primitive chants and ritual cries settled down into the recognizable pattern of words, the static crystallizations of the memory dominated the emerging linguistic structures, for, as Whitehead pointed out, "the essence of language is that it utilizes those elements in experience most easily abstracted for conscious entertainment, and most easily reproduced in experience."[10] Utterances representing entire situation complexes were gradually broken down into movable fragments that represented persisting things or events in the outer world. Thus was born the primary "part of speech" in Indo-European languages, the noun, which has been defined as the name of a person, place, or thing.

It is impossible to determine the relation of language to thought in its initial stages, and this includes the impossibility of fixing causative order to these developments. What can be seen, however, is the profound influence that language exerts on perception and thinking. No matter how flexible sensory and conceptual processes may have been before language began, vast ranges of that flexibility were forever ruled out once experience was forced into words. For those words established the grooves and outlines of man's thinking, so that, on the principle of biological efficiency, his mind ceased to concern itself with experience that could not be easily formulated. Nouns emphasized static outlines and distinctions at the expense of process and interlocking relationships, so that continuity, transaction, and gestalts were gradually overlooked. In effect, nouns developed a perceptual and conceptual *emphasis* that structured man's entire psychology.

Yet man was still aware of process and change, sometimes painfully so, as when he discovered the weakening of his own hands and the graying of his hair—and he struggled to find a way of expressing this in words. One of the ways he did this was through the development of event words, which we call verbs. Nouns and verbs grew up together and were most probably used in conjunction from the beginning, so that the verb evolved as something that "happens to" something else we call a noun. Thus we say that "trees grow," "rain falls," or "man passes away." To a degree, the *processive,* transactional aspects of nature became something that happened to the *static* aspects of nature, and the basic Indo-European unit of expression became the sentence, containing a noun and a verb.

But even the combination of static and dynamic in the noun and the verb failed to capture the full process of living reality. There was more to the rivers and forests, beasts and men, than visible stillness (nouns) and visible movement (verbs), joined together. The primary duality of thought itself—the awareness of the self as a subject over against the known object, the recognition of mental power and its issuance in physical action—led man to wonder about the deep-flowing powers of nature. He saw his own tools and urban technology as "caused" and "directed" by his own thought and planning, and he envisaged nature structured in a similar fashion. The processes of nature came to be regarded as directed by another group of "things" approximating what we call spirit. Thus the earlier, animistic view of nature, which saw everything as alive, was transformed into a static universe of dead "things" activated by a living world of "spirit." Yet the primary structure of language laid down the pattern for every conceptual innovation, so that the world of "spirits" was given the status of nouns in speech, along with the qualities of permanence and solidity that derive from concrete things. Later, as these animistic "spirits" were further abstracted from nature, they became a pantheon of controlling gods who were—because of the permanence of the noun—unchanging and everlasting.

Thus the animating principle of the world was removed to a *super*natural realm "above" the static world of nature. Paradoxically, this attempt to account for change resulted in another unchanging world; indeed, its real feature was its rock-hard permanence. The world became a duality of "matter" and "spirit"; man became a duality of "body" and "soul"; and "mind" became, in Gilbert Ryle's phrase, "the ghost in the machine."[11] Subsequently, the metaphysical problem of Western philosophy was to put these dualities back together without reduction or loss. But science has continued to fragment the world, its method being "divide and conquer," so that reality has now been reduced to a heap of bouncing bits, all relegated to different disciplines under the empirical reign of departments and agencies. This incompatibility of opposites was the straitjacket imposed on the mind of man by language. From the moment that nature became a duality, the unified vision of life has remained an insoluble puzzle, desperately desired but beyond reach.

At the roots of language, therefore, there lies a world view; as W. M. Urban has put it, language is "metaphysized."[12] In sophisticated philosophy, "abstract" nouns involve no reference to physical content or spatial position. Early man, however, lacking such sophistication, imagined spirits to have shape and size and a real world of their own, which he located above himself. As this spatially organized cosmos developed in Hebrew thinking, and as it was elaborated by medieval cosmologists, it became a vertical hierarchy of "places" ranging from the chaotic burning deeps of hell below to the divine Kingdom of God above. Man existed in the middle, sharing in both worlds, aspiring upward to the Kingdom of Heaven, but always in danger of being dragged into the pits of everlasting fire.

Jesus technically overthrew the spatially organized universe when he asserted that "the kingdom of God is within" (Luke 17:21, KJV), pointing to the meaning of the Kingdom in psychological, emotional, and personal terms. But, theology has continued to struggle with spatial cosmology. As Bishop Robinson points out, we may think we have passed beyond spatial literalism, but *"in place of a God who is literally or physically 'up there' we have accepted, as part of our mental furniture, a God who is spiritually or metaphysically 'out there'."*[13] Language constrains us to think along metaphysical grooves laid down in the primeval forest when man first used words for his thoughts.

The spatially organized universe of nature and supernature is, as noted, absolutely fundamental to theology. Because the Hebraic-Christian mind visualized the world this way, theology has centered on *the assertion of relationships* between these realms. Precisely how this assertion has been done, and exactly how the Indo-European noun-verb sentence pattern was utilized in these assertions, is a fascinating study—and a highly revealing one for the light it sheds on the nature of theology itself.

In the Christian tradition the separation of the seamless robe of the universe into God, man, and nature was only the beginning of a total fragmentation. The classificatory power of the noun gave man the tools to further divide nature into "realms" or "kingdoms" that were a projection of his own political structure onto the universe at large. Christian cosmologists imagined a hierarchy of power extending from the King of Kings at the top, down through the various levels of creation—a kind of divine monarchy. This structure persisted right through the Middle Ages, receiving philosophical support from Platonic and Neo-platonic thought and artistic expression in the works of Dante and Milton. But to understand the way in which theology used symbolic language to *unite* these different realms is to grasp its whole dynamic.

Nature, that part of the world which is not man, is a neutral world classifiable into *animal, vegetable,* and *mineral.* (The italicized words, here and following, refer to the table on page 77.) Culture and civilization are forms of human activity which transform a subhuman, amoral nature into something with human shape and meaning. The first step for urban man was to fence off (Divide and conquer!) a section of the *vegetable* world to form a *farm* or *garden,* and part of the *animal* world to form a *herd* or *flock* of domesticated animals. The *mineral* world was chipped and hewn and dragged away, and a *city* was constructed, adorned with refined minerals. And, because of the need for fresh *water,* the earliest civilizations grew up beside the great *rivers* of the Afro-Asian landmass—the Nile, the Tigris-Euphrates, and the Indus. The raw world of nature was thus transformed into the idealized, artificial world of urban settlement—flock, garden, and city, beside the river. And it was here that the scattered *human* realm first took on its idealized form, a *society of men.*

Above the world of nature was the realm of *spirits,* who were likewise organized into a society of *spirits,* like the dryads and naiads of Greek religion and the angels of Christianity. And finally, as man's powers of abstraction increased, men imagined a *divine* realm "above" the spiritual, organized into a *society of gods,* like the Olympian pantheon of the Greeks or the Vedic gods of India. The civilized form of nature, though designed by men, was long regarded as the work of the gods. Thus human govern-

ments were modeled on divine government, and human
laws were passed down from "on high." Moreover, the
divine powers had to be thanked for flock and garden, so
that the firstfruits of harvest and roundup were offered up
in sacrifice.

Christian tradition developed an elaborate symbolic
structure upon these seven realms, the outlines of which
are easily discovered in Biblical mythology. At the time
of their creation, Adam and Eve were placed in a *garden,*
the sacred focal point of which was the *tree of life.* The
sacrificial system of the Hebrews required that the best
lamb of the *flock* be offered up to God, an act which
sanctified the whole God-given flock. Moreover, at the
center of the *city* there stood the sacred building, the
temple, dedicated to the worship of the divine. Every
pantheon of gods is soon ruled by one god: Indra became
supreme in the Vedic pantheon by supplanting Varuna;
Zeus rose by overthrowing Cronus; Yahweh became the
one God by conquering Baal, god of the Moabites and
the Midianites, and Ashtoreth, goddess of the Phoenicians.
Thus, the *one God* became the focal point of the divine,
and the *Spirit,* who first appears "moving over the face of
the waters" at Creation (Gen. 1:2), became the focal
point of the *spiritual* realm. And finally, there is the sacred
river of life, which is linked with the four rivers of Eden
and the river flowing from beneath God's throne in the
New Jerusalem (Gen. 2:10; Rev. 22:1). The concrete
reference point was the Jordan, where Jesus was baptized;
hence the symbol for the sacred river is the *baptismal
water.*

The full array of these symbols is set out in the following
table. The apocalyptic symbols represent focal points of
the sacred—specific "things" in each of the realms where
the power of the divine is disclosed or revealed.

TABLE

THE SEVEN NATURAL REALMS	THE SEVEN IDEALIZED REALMS OF CIVILIZATION	APOCALYPTIC SYMBOLS
1 divine	society of gods	one God
2 spiritual	society of spirits	one Spirit
3 human	society of men	Christ
4 animal	herd, flock	lamb
5 vegetable	farm, garden	tree of life
6 mineral	city	temple
7 water	river	baptismal water

Biblical religion establishes relationships between these separate realms by *linking them symbolically*. The central symbol in Christianity is *Christ,* the one man in whom the divine is revealed, and who is historically identified with Jesus of Nazareth. Christ brings cosmic redemption, which is conveyed in Biblical religion as a reuniting of all the separate levels of the universe. The only linguistic method available for expressing this is metaphor, which simply asserts that one thing *is* another. Thus in fully developed Biblical symbolism, "God *is* spirit" (John 4:24), "Jesus Christ *is* Lord" (Phil. 2:11; Rom. 1:4; I Cor. 8:6), and "the Lord *is* the Spirit" (II Cor. 3:17) (italics added)— metaphorical identifications that form the basis of the doctrines of the incarnation and Trinity. Moreover, Christ *is* the Lamb of God (John 1:29), uniting the human and animal realms, and the tree of life or the vine of which we are the branches (John 15:5), uniting the human and the vegetable. Christ *is,* furthermore, the "cornerstone, in whom the whole structure is joined together" (Eph. 2:20–21), and the temple that was to be rebuilt in three days turns out to be his risen body. We are brought into new life "in Christ" by baptism in the water of life, which makes us "members of his body" (Eph. 5:30), and by the Eucharist, the eating of two vegetable products, bread and wine, which are said *to be* the body and blood of the Lamb, who is also the bread of life and the water of life (John 6:35; 4:14).

Thus Paul finds Christ to be the focal point of the whole cosmos: "Therein lies the richness of God's free grace lavished upon us, imparting full wisdom and insight. He has made known to us his hidden purpose—such was his will and pleasure determined beforehand in Christ—to be put into effect when the time was ripe: namely, *that the universe, all in heaven and on earth, might be brought into a unity in Christ."* (Eph. 1:7–10, NEB, italics added.) For, as Paul wrote in another letter, in Christ "all things are held together" (Col. 1:17, NEB).

These metaphorical statements about Christ, and about this world's relationship to the world "above," are made in the context of man's existential problems: the feeling of limitation, the inner gnawing of guilt, and the need for security in an uncertain world. In the face of these fragmenting forces these affirmations about Christ constitute a redeeming answer. What they affirm, specifically, is that the divisions of the world and the gulf between "heaven" and "earth" are only apparent, not real. The metaphorical linking of symbols accomplishes a symbolic *reintegration* of the whole universe in the central symbol, Christ. And, through man's participation in Christ, he is linked to the Godhead.

There is no way that man's link with the divine can be *logically* proved; it is therefore expressed grammatically by metaphor. Theology, properly conceived, must resist any attempt to reduce metaphor to simile, to say that

Christ is *like* God, for this misses the unitive function of metaphor. Moreover, theology must resist the attempt to build logical doctrines upon metaphor, such as the doctrine that Jesus is a "sacrifice" to God, based on the metaphor that Jesus *is* the Lamb of God. Metaphor is not fact. There is thus no way to prove that the doctrines of incarnation or Trinity are literally so, or that the bread and wine of the Eucharist are literally the body and blood of Jesus.

Theology has not only failed to see that its statements are metaphorical assertions of unity, the integration of the various "realms"; it has also failed to grasp that the universe of "realms" is itself a metaphor, an image of the universe based on the political structure of human society. Since theology is dealing with metaphors within a metaphor, it is no wonder it is confused.

The greatest problems of theology have centered on explaining the meaning of metaphorical relationships. How are the "divine" and "human" realms connected? In what sense is Christ both God and man? How does man experience God? Yet underlying all of these, and underlying the whole structure of Christianity, is the metaphysical assumption that the "divine" and "human" realms are *separate,* and this is in turn the unconscious metaphysic of language. The awesome union of spirit and matter in the being of man has been split asunder by the reification of words; process and transaction have been frozen in their tracks. The intangible, burning spark of life moving through all things has been "thingified"—ossified into a spirit from somewhere else—until man's representation of it has been frozen in static symbolism. The beautiful fabric of nature, woven of water and star dust and organized into animal and vegetable in a total ecological harmony, has been broken into a collection of unrelated bits. Can these dry bones be made to live?

They can live if we take the world in its wholeness, realizing that there is no need to *uni*fy what is already one. Wittgenstein defined the method when he said, *"Look and see,"* and again, "Don't think, but look!"[14] Observe and describe. And a new language, which avoids the fragmenting effect of the noun, is precisely what is needed—a language of description. This new language must necessarily reveal the relationships between things; it must capture harmony rather than separate notes; it must highlight the living process rather than static abstractions. It is clear that vast problems exist within the Western languages, problems too great to be solved by anything short of a radical experiment with language itself. Such a solution calls in question the basic assumptions of the entire Indo-European civilization, on the basis of the demonstrable fact that these assumptions are too small for the infinite mystery of the universe.

4

A Radical Experiment

Culture is man's total way of looking at the world and himself. In a personal sense, culture is an attitude of mind, the residue of all the knowledge the mind has possessed, the traces of experience. In a broader sense, it is a world view passed on from generation to generation through unconscious mental absorption. But culture finally stretches right back into biology and the evolutionary past that laid down the channels of thinking and acting none can escape. As such, culture merges with basic assumptions.

A few dozen million years ago, when man was little more than a tree-climbing primate, the possibilities for thought were clearly present in the roots of the brain. Previously confined with black-and-white vision, the creature that would someday become man, for some unknown reason, took to the trees. There he found himself in a colorful arboreal world where survival depended on distinguishing poisonous fruits from edible ones, and on estimating jumping distances yards wide between the trees. With his nose now a long way from the ground, the sense of smell gradually waned and in its place emerged panchromatic, binocular vision capable of distinguishing hundreds of shades of color, and eventually performing distance-judging tricks such as hitting a baseball moving just under one hundred miles per hour. Arboreal preman—long before the development of toolmaking or even bipedal, running feet—was developing the equipment for the *visual* discovery of the world, a discovery that continues with microscopes, telescopes, and spectroscopes today.

The basis of culture is a set of patterns in the brain, and they are laid along visual lines. No theory of man, education, society, or language can afford to ignore this fact. Thus the emergence of urbanized man and linguistic man went hand in hand with the emergence of imaginative man —man the image maker. His perceived and described world became a spatial pattern of concretely imagined "realms," a projection of human society upon the cosmos. Moreover, the visual habits of man, reinforced by the spatial organization of the noun, left him with a peculiar feeling of being alone, cut off from the matrix of his birth. It was to this psychic schism, projected onto the universe at large, that religion addressed itself, seeking always to hitch man's vision to the stars. For religion seeks to show man's continuity with the rest of the world, to show his linkage with the gods, and to make his *ex-istence,* his "coming out" in the world, finally meaningful.

Running through all of culture is language, which crystallizes that culture and determines its directions in startling and subtle ways. Language is to culture what thread is to fabric, determining the pattern and texture, the durability and richness of the whole cloth. This is so because thought tends to be linguistic and men studiously avoid thinking in other ways, allowing themselves to be bound, as Susanne Langer suggests, to "a tiny grammar-bound island, in the midst of a sea of feeling."[1] Man's images of the universe, carved in the wood of this world, are always subject to the unalterable limits of linguistic thinking. If the language structure is divisive—if its categories are applied to the whole of reality, and if that reality is regarded as explainable with words—then theology must be pursued within those self-imposed limits.

In a very important sense, knowledge is impossible without language to communicate and record it, and the scientific knowledge we pride ourselves in is impossible without a language which divides space into "things" and time into "events." Separation is the key to the isolation of variables. But, in another sense, knowledge of this kind is precisely what brings on the Fall of man. For unfallen man was preliterate man in the magical forest, completely at one with nature and God, who came walking in Eden "in the cool of the day" (Gen. 3:8). The eating of the forbidden fruit, however, brought self-awareness (We had better wear fig leaves!), separation from God (You must *leave* the Garden!), and the knowledge of Good and Evil, that is, the knowledge of opposites. Deprived of union with God, man found himself in a divided world of wilderness and Garden, Egypt and Canaan, the "city of the earth" and the City of God. It was the first step, but it led to the broken world of church and state, spirit and flesh, supernature and nature, and finally to rival ways of viewing the whole thing —religion and science. And all of this enshrined in a divisive language structure that left man with a tattered universe. His paltry equations and creeds are but ludicrous attempts to catch the lost wonder.

In one sense salvation is a return to the past, to a kind of Garden-of-Eden union with the divine. This idealization of the past crops up in much secular thinking, as in the romantic idea of the "noble savage," the Victorian revival of the Middle Ages, and the Marxist notion of a primitive classless society—that is, a society that has not yet been divided. In another sense the desire for salvation is a yearning toward a future in which harmony will be restored, where man will come back, so to speak, to the throne of God. The so-called American Dream, "the orgiastic future that year by year recedes before us,"[2] shares something of both views. But finally, salvation is accomplished by Christ, in whom "all things are held to-gether" (Col. 1:17, NEB). In him is "the pattern of all the heavenly" (I Cor. 15:48, NEB). In him all divisions between God and the world are healed—as the Council of Chalcedon put it, "WITHOUT CONFUSION, WITHOUT CHANGE, WITHOUT DIVISION, WITHOUT SEPARATION."[3]

There is a sense in which the historical emphasis of Christianity makes salvation impossible. For the age of Eden, the union with God in heaven, and the harmony of all things in Christ, as *historical* events, are events *in* the past or *in* the future and therefore not in the present. But salvation, if it is to mean anything real to the believer, must be attainable on earth, *now*. Here we arrive at the second linguistic problem of theology: not only has language fragmented the universe spatially into a political hierarchy of "realms"; it has also strung out the saving events of God's incursion into human life over the scattered pages of a dead history. Even if Christ was the unity of all things, even if the incarnation was "God with us," how can we be sure that God is still with us? What importance does a single event in history have for man today, or three thousand years from now, or three million? What is the *connection* between *then* and *now?* How does a temporal event of the past guarantee eternal life? Must we wait for eternal life to come at the end of time, building our present life on expectation and hope?

Whatever "eternal life" may be, it is the heart of reli-gious experience, Christian or otherwise. Yet to grasp the meaning of eternal life we must think about time, the real time where life is lived. But here again we run against the limits of language. For just as the spatial patterns of language fail to cope with the continuity of nature, so too do the temporal patterns of language fail to capture that time which is eternal.

Time is a mystery. What is this invisible fluid which engulfs all things? We measure time by the passage of the earth round the sun, dividing it into days and "moons," ignoring the fact that the division is not exact. And this time is relative in a baffling sort of way. On the moon a day lasts a month and is confused with a year, for the moon circles the earth once a month and makes only one spin in the circuit. And today is the first New Year's Day on Neptune since the days of Napoleon. Time is measured by the motion of our planet and that motion is chosen because it makes sense of man's life and is verifiable in his experience. Yet what is time measured by the rotation of a galaxy (one turn every 200 million years) or the rotation of an electron (6,570 thousand million pulsations every second)? In the long view, time is an imponderable, stretching away in both directions, time out of mind, until the mind is bent and dazzled by the unimaginable. But this is the clue for which we seek. Whatever is inconceivable is beyond the power of thought and language, and quite meaningless when hammered into a pattern of words. Whatever it means, man finds himself moving on a journey through a time that has no beginning and can have no ending, and he is lost in a vastness he cannot understand.

But all of this has little bearing on the living time of the mind, a time that has almost no relation to clocks and calendars. Here time is measured not by a pendulum swing but by the beating of a heart, and the ebb and flow of air within the lungs. At birth the human heart beats 140 times a minute but it eventually levels out at about half that rate. Moreover, men are somehow aware of the change, for youthful days are fast and full but the sense of time as adults has us all watching the clock.

The time of the mind has a magic all its own. Here the barriers come down, for the mind can range over sea and mountain and all of time, even to the farthest stars, oblivious to time. And during sleep, time seems to stop, except for the dance of dream, which is as much forgotten as remembered. Yet this is very close to the secret, for time is related to what is going on, so that when events cease and motion stops the mysterious flow of time is stilled. An eternity where nothing happens is no time at all, and one crowded hour of glorious life can make all the difference. For time is change and change is time, and when the youthful flurry of life is gone the time hangs heavy on our hearts.

It may be impossible to say what time *is,* but it is apparent that the only real time is present time, for that is the only "place" where change occurs. Future time is present anticipation and past time is a residue in the memory. But present time somehow moves along with man or man moves with it, or perhaps we are fooled by the idea of moving in time, so that all we can say is that the movement of time is unique. The past was "present" when it occurred, the future will not occur until it is "present." The long line of time is best seen as a recurring present, and the unity of time is the fusion that takes place in the *now* of human memory and imagination.

Time's secret, then, is so close that we miss it while scanning the record of the past. Yet it is precisely this scanning which gives us the sensation of time, for the changes we see produce the record of change called time. We are fooled into thinking time is "out there." But time is our own moving attention, our changing situation, the vision of the passing dance and shadow of existence. What then is the present moment? Can it be captured and held up to the light? Can we tell where it starts and ends? Here is *the* mystery of time. Try as we may, we cannot capture a present moment, for it eludes us like gossamer. Once captured, it is in the past. It cannot be observed; it can only be lived through—in fact we can live in no other place but now. But try to define it and the starting point merges with the end point and the whole instant between the limits vanishes. Yet it is here, closer to us than we are to ourselves, but totally beyond observation or words. The present moment exists but cannot be "timed" and so it is itself timeless. The timeless now is the eternal moment where all living happens, and thus eternal life is here and now and nowhere else. In Paul Tillich's words, "man, in the Christian view, comes from the eternal and goes to the eternal; and he can experience the eternal in every moment of time. . . . Eternal life is *life* . . . , the eternal now."[4] The eternal now is the "gospel according to this moment," as Thoreau put it, and eternal life is life in "the nick of time."[5]

The eternal life offered by Jesus has been perverted in the popular mind into endless life—living forever and ever, even beyond the grave. Yet those who anxiously ask where they will *be* after death might ask themselves another question: where they *were* before birth. At once both questions collapse as nonsense. And if we look at endless life from another point of view, the whole notion turns into a nightmare. For endless life means either doing something or doing nothing—forever. And who can imagine anything he would like to do forever? Eat endless plates of filet mignon, ice cream, and cherries jubilee? Unlimited beer and skittles? An endless night with the Playmate of the Year? Singing round the throne of God forever? An endless life of any of these would make one *die* of boredom.

Once we are released from the hell of everlasting life in heaven, we are open to the reality of eternal life in the

now. We can live with quiet attention to what is immediate;
we live at what T. S. Eliot called "the still point of the
turning world"; existence unfolds in an ecstatic *"peak-
experience,"* which Abraham Maslow describes as *"a
self-validating, self-justifying moment which carries its own
intrinsic value with it."*[6] Perhaps our world should be populated like Aldous Huxley's world in *Island,* with myna
birds to call us back to reality: "Here and now, boys, here
and now. Attention." Any other way of living is pointless,
for man is neither a human "has-been" nor a human
"will-be" but a human "be-*ing*." To live in the past or the
future is to sell oneself to a continual be-*coming* or an
imaginary be-*leaving*—for believing is faith in what *might*
be or *could* be, but not what *is*.

When Moses confronted the burning bush, he asked:
"If I come to the people of Israel and say to them, 'The
God of your fathers has sent me to you,' and they ask me,
'What is his name?' what shall I say to them?" The reply
out of the bush ignored Moses' talk of the God of the
fathers, which was a return to a dead past: "I AM WHO I
AM. . . . Say this to the people of Israel, 'I AM has sent me
to you.' " (Ex. 3:13–14.) God is a present God who pro-
claims himself as I AM. Thus Jesus said to the Jews, "Truly,
truly, I say to you, before Abraham was, I am." (John
8:58.) For the incarnation takes place at time zero, the
dividing point of time symbolic of the timeless now where
past and future meet. But theology has fixed the incarnation
to a datable time in the past where it cannot touch today.

Eternal truth is timeless truth, truth about the present
moment. But in theology, truth is built instead on historical
events: the timeless has given way to the temporal. The
unspeakable meaning of eternal life has been frozen into
words, ossified into statements about what happened instead of what happens. But what theology has failed to

grasp is that, while making Christianity hinge on historical events, it has failed to clarify what distinguishes *these* historical events from any others. In what ways are the historical words of Jesus more important than the historical words of Confucius, Aristotle, Shakespeare, or Mao Tse-tung? Thus the historical emphasis of traditional theology equates timeless truths with mere historical events, such as wars and feuds and empires, in much the same way that the application of nouns to the divine brings the infinite down to the world of mere "things." Western man, in the bind of time and space, has conceived a God who is also in the bind of time and space, or worse, in the bind of nouns and verbs.

It is no wonder, then, that we live in a time of the death of God. The divine dimension has been spatialized to a realm beyond, and its connections with this world have been temporalized, and thus flung away to a dead past. *Theo-logy,* that is, God-talk, has removed God, leaving us alone on a lower plane, at a dead end of history where the mysteries of life have been given over to the mythology of scientism. The destruction of timeless truth by language has led some philosophers to call an end to all God talk. T. R. Miles, for example, has recommended "the way of silence qualified by parables."[7] The plight of theology calls for a radical solution, for "the way of silence," even if "qualified by parables," seems like a retreat into obscurantism. The final question becomes, then, a last-ditch attempt to salvage theology: Is religious language possible? Is God talk possible without either running up against the factual domain of empirical science or destroying the very truth of which we wish to speak? Or must we say nothing?

A new theological language must necessarily avoid the limitations of "things" and "events," which precludes an Indo-European solution. But I believe a startling solution lies waiting in the work of the American anthropologist Benjamin Lee Whorf (1897–1941).

Whorf is known for a relatively small corpus of linguistic studies that deal with the way human thinking is shaped by language. Again and again Whorf found, through studying the language and culture of the American Indians, that many of their cultural traits were closely related to the structure of their languages. In essence, this principle of *linguistic relativity* "holds that all observers are not led by the same physical evidence to the same picture of the universe, unless their linguistic backgrounds are similar, or can in some way be calibrated."[8] English can be calibrated with other Indo-European languages—Latin, Greek, Russian, German, Dutch, French, Spanish, Italian, Welsh, Polish, Swedish, Sanskrit, Pali, and numerous relatives of these—but it cannot be calibrated with most non-Indo-European tongues.

Our own immersion in the Indo-European language structure and its particular modes of thought leads us to regard our own view of the world as "normal"—and shared by everyone else. That anyone should actually *see* the world and describe it differently comes as a revelation. But Whorf made it clear that our own grammatical structure, which we identify with "common sense," is chiefly valuable as a means of communicating with those who share our system. Language is a social tool, a fact that says nothing about its value as a philosophical, mathematical, theological, or any other kind of tool. What we call common sense has no *necessary* basis in the real world that language is used to describe. As Whorf put it:

> We cut up and organize the spread and flow of events as we do, largely because, through our mother tongue, we are parties to an agreement to do so, not because nature is segmented in exactly that way for all to see.

Languages differ not only in how they build their sentences but also in how they break down nature to secure the elements to put in those sentences.[9]

Whorf's conclusions lead to a fascinating possibility. Since the main requirement of a new theological language is that it be without the limitations of nouns and verbs, is there any existing culture exhibiting a totally different language structure from which a new language might be derived? As soon as the question is raised, a possibility looms large, for Whorf's studies centered on the Hopi Indian language, a language as different from Indo-European as diamond is from coal. And the comparison is apt, for the cultural achievements of the Hopi radiate a compelling glitter that eclipses our own.

The Indian population of the Americas, including the Arctic Eskimos, was of Asiatic origin, having come across the land bridge above the Pacific before it sank into the Bering Strait. When this migration began is difficult to know, but the last of these migrants probably completed the journey some twenty thousand years ago. From Alaska they spread southward, adapting as they went, throughout the entire Americas, driven forward by the pressure of increasing northern migrants, and, if Thor Heyerdahl is correct, some of them may have drifted back across the southern Pacific on huge rafts, coming close to rejoining their long lost brothers in the South Sea Islands. New as America is, the uncharted shores found by the Vikings, and later by Columbus, were populated whole millennia before Babylon was dreamed of.

The ancestors of the American Indians were thus separated from Eurasia when European cavemen were still chipping conveniently shaped stones into crude cutters and scrapers. With more time on their hands than twice the entire record of history, the Indians had unique opportuni-

ties for developing a distinctive culture apart from their
Eurasian contemporaries. It is therefore no surprise that
their languages reflect entirely different visions of the
world from those of the Indo-Europeans. The background
of European man is fraught with disturbing change:
England was forged out of half a dozen invasions, and most
of Europe has been engulfed by foreign culture at least a
dozen times in the last three thousand years. It comes as a
surprise to learn that the Hopi tribe have occupied the same
plateau for some five thousand years, and that their life
differs little from what it was that long ago. Whatever else
it means, it bodes well that they have fitted into the scheme
of things so early, so well, for so long.

Through most of their history the Hopi villages have
been well isolated from syncretistic influences, high in the
mountains of sunny Arizona. From the beginning, the
Hopi have lived on seeds and small game, a fragile existence wrung from a harsh environment. Water is scarce,
mountain springs are unreliable, drought is frequent—
along with sandstorms, flashflooding, winter frost, pesty
rodents, and, since the arrival of the white man, the debil-
itating effects of European culture, Mennonite missionary
zeal, and Caucasian disease. Apart from the modern breakdown of Hopi culture since contact was first made with the
Spaniards, the Hopi exhibit a cultural adaptation that seems
to have remained at about the level of the Old Stone Age.
As such, they come close to a model of preliterate man,
man who was one with his surroundings in a manner we
have quite forgotten.

Being one with nature means making no effort to distinguish oneself from it. Thus the Hopi feel and live as part
of the pattern of nature, entwined with the wind and water,
in mind as well as body. Everything that nature does has
relevance to man and every thought of man moves out into

the surrounding hills. There are no imaginary "things" in the Hopi world: his world is one of *actual* cornstalks and sheep herds. Thinking about these cornstalks and sheep herds has as much effect on the Hopi as watering the corn or tending the sheep would have, so that mental energy has an importance quite unknown to us. The Hopi therefore exhibit a remarkable intensity, a determination to harmonize thought with action, a desire to move with the cosmic forces of the universe. Indeed, this integrating of mental energy and physical action is part of the larger integration of religious life and secular life, though the Hopi would not distinguish the two. Thus Hopi religion is linked with common labor, political organization, social structure, and mutual survival—a unitive life-style that blends all human activity into a single pattern of interdependence.

What is fundamental here is the Hopi world view and its remarkable relationship with the structure of their language, for here is to be found a possible solution to many problems, theological and otherwise. The Hopi Indian actually sees the world of "things" quite differently from Indo-European man. Only relatively long, enduring events come out as anything like nouns in Hopi; events of short duration that we would classify as nouns—lightning, wave, flame, or smoke puff—are necessarily verbs. Yet even with the Hopi noun there is a difference. Indo-European languages have so spatialized the universe, in thought and in seeing, that nouns are always self-contained "things" occupying something called space. Things are, as Aristotle said in his *Metaphysics,* a duality of form and matter.[10] We make no distinction for obviously shaped things like tables and chairs and trees, but anything the shape of which is indefinite requires that we apply a shape. Thus we tend to designate them with a shape: a *glass* of water, *cup* of coffee, *stick* of wood, or *lump* of dough. It is considered rather sloppy to ask for "a beer" or even "a coffee," and completely beyond our thinking to ask for "a water." But, for the Hopi, who does not distinguish container from contained, nor form from matter, to ask for "a water" is the normal way of dealing with the fuzziest of "things."

This simple difference, however, points to a larger and more significant difference. Unconscious of spatial distinctions, the Hopi lacks any notion of imaginary space, and consequently of imaginary "things" to put in it. Reality is utterly concrete. Thus, the spatial fragmentation of the living flux into something called matter and something called spirit, which activates matter, is impossible in his thinking and speaking. The reason for this lack of spatial distinctions is that Hopi is primarily a language of verbs. Short-term "things" come out as "happenings," and the basic sentence pattern consists of a verb.

Yet even here there is a difference. Indo-European verbs refer to distinct "events" strung out along a line or road. These "events"—making up the past, present, and future—have an unusual kind of reality to them, so that the passage of time is seen either as "life's journey" along the road of time or as a kind of march of "events" past a fixed observer, as when we say the days are "rolling by." This view is really a translation of time into spatial terms, so that we refer to time in terms of *length* or *distance:* a "long" time, a "short" time, the "remote" past, or the "near" future. This translation of time into space entails a translation of "events" into something more like "things," strung out in sequence like a row of bottles. Well-developed memories, extensive written records, calendars, and the ability to plan and predict the future with a measure of accuracy have reinforced this spatial view of time. But, in the process, "events" have taken on a quality of thinginess, a kind of solid reality that engrosses us. And, in the extreme, it enslaves us, leading our attention into the past or into the future—away from the present.

The Hopi verb system, however, reflects a totally different view of time. The Hopi verb is organized around two tenses, the "manifested" and the "manifesting."[11] There is no spatial translation involved, since both verb tenses capture *actual activity*. The "manifested" tense includes both our past and present tenses, since what *has* happened or *is* happening are both manifested fact in the present moment. The "manifesting" tense includes the English future, but only the future as viewed from the present moment, for the future is always manifesting itself in the present as a possibility, an expectation, or a hope. Both tenses, then, are placed squarely *in the present,* which is viewed as a focal point—a point where the past is accumulated and from which the future will spring. Hopi verbs, therefore, do not lead the speaker to think of the past and future as real. The only real time for him is the *now,* and his grammar forces him to express and see everything in terms of present activity.

A further difference in Hopi verbs is the distinction between "aspects."[12] The "punctual" or the "segmentative" aspect of the verb is used depending on the kind of activity being described. A Hopi Indian using a knife to cut something would use the manifested tense to describe the action of cutting, since it would be a cutting going on. If he wanted to refer to the "point" of the knife, for which we use a noun, he would use the "punctual" aspect, which is used to describe a single localized action. He would describe it as a kind of "pointing." Confronted with the blade of a saw, he would not think in terms of spatial extension, but in terms of a whole series of "pointings," a row of segmented actions. He would use the "segmentative" aspect of the verb, formed by adding a double reduplication. The words he

would use would be *ho' 'ci* ("pointing") and *hoci' cita*
("pointings" or "zigzaggings"). A few more examples of
this language follow:

ENGLISH	HOPI	
NOUN	"PUNCTUAL" VERB	"SEGMENTATIVE" VERB
fringe	*ca' mi* (slashed in from the edge)	*cami' mita* (fringed, slashed into a fringe at the edge)
wave	*wa' la* (makes a wave, gives a slosh)	*wala' lata* (tossing in waves, kicking up a sea)
sparkle	*rï' 'pi* (gives a flash, flashes)	*rïpi' pita* (sparkles, sparkling)
fire	*ʔi' wi* (flames up)	*ʔiwi' wita* (flaming up, a fire)
thunder	*ʔi' mï* (explodes, goes off like a gun)	*ʔïmï' mïta* (thundering)

This use of verbs is foreign to our way of thinking, and
the translations of Hopi words look cumbersome indeed,
since most of our translations involve a noun. But for the
Hopi these words are part of his everyday speaking, and
they bring his world to life with continual action, movement, and vibration. His language constrains him to think
of "things" as "happenings," events-in-the-process-of-
eventing, so that he notices action and process where Indo-
European man finds only a dead world of stillness.

Classical Newtonian physics may be considered as an
extension of Indo-European language patterns—the laws
governing "things" in uniform space, moving through
linear time. Modern physics, however, is built upon con-

cepts like energetic particles ("wavicles") and fields of vibration. Since these concepts have no grammatical equivalents, they disturb our "common sense." Scientists, however, have become accustomed to working with these new ideas and have devised new mathematical languages to cope with them. The operations of differential and integral calculus, for example, are methods of dealing with changing situations or processes involving known laws and limits, where mechanical principles no longer apply. But, as Whorf pointed out, the Hopi language has a built-in "calculus"—grammatical structures attuned to energetic pattern and process—suggesting that it may well be the logical choice for a process language. L. L. Whyte apparently never explored this possibility, although, as long ago as 1948, he suggested that "the next development in man" would have to be a language of process that would fit the new vision of the world discovered by twentieth-century science.[13]

Every meaningful sentence in the Indo-European languages *must* have at least a noun and a verb, expressed or implied. Thus, as Whorf noted, "we are constantly reading into nature fictional acting entities, simply because our verbs must have substantives in front of them."[14] We say, "*It* is snowing," or "*It* looks like rain," creating a linguistic ghost to fill up the subject slot of the sentence. We say, "A light flashed," creating an actor, "light," to perform the action, "flashed"; whereas the Hopi language uses a single word, *rĭ"pi*—"flash," or "flashing." From the Hopi point of view, the noun and verb are inseparable: there can be no light without a flashing and no flashing without a light.

The Whorfian hypothesis actually calls in question the whole Indo-European metaphysic, including all the philosophies that spring from it. Aristotelian "logic," for example, constructed on the subject-verb sentence pattern, falls to pieces in Hopi grammar. Plato's world of Ideas, founded on the Permanence of nouns—Beauty, Truth, Goodness—likewise collapses. Modern secular man, who is at war with transcendence, theism, and supernaturalism, is at war with his own linguistic conventions, those basic assumptions which not only make God talk possible but force all statements into patterns that are out of step with the living world of experience. Revisionary theology is a perpetual failure, for it always smuggles the same metaphysic back into the system. Theology, therefore, like most Western philosophy, consumes most of its space *qualifying* its statements so they will not be misleading. (A brief but instructive example is the Council of Chalcedon formulation of the incarnation. See Chapter 6.) Theology has therefore become a ponderous set of dogmatics or systematics that (apart from being too heavy to hold) conceals the essentials in a huge morass of qualifications.

Bonhoeffer's call for secular talk of God was a daring call, but the answer is no less daring. What is required is a radical abandonment of traditional language structures, an abandonment that took place long ago in advanced physics and biology. Could a new theological language not dispense with the subject-predicate structure and thereby avoid the dualistic metaphysic of Indo-European thinking? For there is no demonstrable reason why theological statements must have a "subject" and a "predicate." There is no reason why we should not abandon "statements" and even "sentences" and look toward a new kind of language game—the meaningful utterance. For Jesus himself often refused direct statement, preferring the language of parable.

The Hopi language suggests a starting point, for it incorporates a unified perception of the world by describing movement, process, and vibratory pattern in the present moment. Such a language structure is necessarily *descriptive* rather than explanatory, and it must necessarily describe the world without explaining it away or reducing it to static abstractions. Alan Watts once remarked that "we can speak of a group of homes as housing without feeling impelled to ask, *'What* is it that is housing?' "[15] Elsewhere he says, "If we can speak of a mat as matting, or of a couch as seating, why can't we think of people as 'peopling,' of brains as 'braining,' or of an ant as an 'ant-ing'?"[16] Other examples leap to mind: planking, siding, railing, building, dwelling, lighting. There is no reason why every *think* must be a *thing*. For, in a world where every event is a "happen-*ing*" and every thing is a "th-*ing*," we must learn to talk of man as "manning," nature as "naturing"—and, perhaps, of God as "godding."

5

The Creating Universe

From the beginning the doctrine of Creation has been the basis of Christian belief and the cornerstone of theology. The Apostles' Creed, accepted almost universally throughout Christendom, begins: "I believe in God the Father Almighty, Maker of heaven and earth." The most unschooled of people who have any idea of God think of him as a Creator, and children tell us that "God made the world" long before they have grasped any other Christian ideas. This theological experiment, then, must begin with Creation, the doctrine on which the rest are built.

Over and over again the pages of the Bible echo with this compelling vision of God as the Maker of all things. "The LORD God formed man of dust from the ground, and breathed into his nostrils the breath of life . . . . And the LORD God planted a garden in Eden, in the east." (Gen. 2:7–8.) "Behold, the Lord was standing beside a wall built with a plumb line, with a plumb line in his hand." (Amos 7:7.) "When he established the heavens, I was there, when he drew a circle on the face of the deep." (Prov. 8:27.) "Thou didst set the earth on its foundations, so that it should never be shaken." (Ps. 104:5.) This Maker is always painted as the architect of the universe, the potter, the gardener, the smith. The concept of the

Maker therefore bears the unmistakable stamp of man's preoccupation with construction, metallurgy, and farming during the early stages of urban civilization.

It is notable that the Genesis account of creation says that God made "the heavens and the earth," suggesting that he is "above" both realms—in Paul Tillich's phrase, he is the "God above God."[1] But elsewhere, God has been brought "down" to the supernatural so that subsequent formulations describe the Creator as God *in heaven* who made the world. It is in this form—symmetrically stated as *"the Creator created the creation"*—that the doctrine will be examined, for this displays the metaphysic adopted by later theology.

In the Indo-European languages, nouns such as "Creator" and "creation" function as if their external referents were distinct and separable "things." A noun isolates a manageable piece from the continuum of experience, rounding off whatever it names from its surroundings. In referring to a wave, for example, we mentally ignore the fact that a "wave" is inseparable from a "trough" and that both are static abstractions from a changing movement of water. This static quality of the concrete noun dominates our grammar, so that abstract nouns follow the same relationships within sentences as do their concrete counterparts. As Bergson put it, "our concepts have been formed on the model of solids; . . . our logic is, pre-eminently, the logic of solids."[2] Thus abstract concepts carry a quality of thinginess. In speaking of "adding insult to injury," for example, the thinginess of "insult" and "injury" leads us to assume that "injury" ends where "insult" begins—that there is no insult involved in injury, or vice versa. If we wish to say that "insult" and "injury" overlap in this particular instance, a qualification to that effect must be added. Yet whether we speak simply of *adding* insult to

injury, or go on to suggest some *overlap,* the thinginess of
our concepts is apparent in the ideas of "adding" and
"overlap." "Creator" and "creation" function in a similar
way, as mutually exclusive "things." They are imagined
as spatially separate: the "Creator" is visualized as being
*super*natural—above the "creation."

The separation between God and the world is overcome
in the doctrines of Christ and the Holy Spirit. God, as
the Word, becomes *one* with the flesh of Jesus, and God as
Spirit permeates the world completely. But theology has
understood the union of Word-and-flesh and the coming
of the Holy Spirit as "events" coming after Creation, later
in history. Thus the doctrine of Creation is always developed from the standpoint of the separation of God and the
world in the beginning, that is, at a point in the past when
the incarnation and coming of the Spirit had not yet occurred.

As already noted, there is no way within the Indo-European languages in which two separate "realms"—"heaven"
and "earth"—can be logically related. The linguistic devices used are therefore not logical but metaphorical or
analogical. Metaphor utilizes the verb *is,* simply asserting
identity: Jesus Christ *is* Lord; the Lord *is* the Spirit. Analogy utilizes a transitive verb and explains the relationship
by a parallel. The device of analogy underlies the myth
of Creation, which asserts that the way in which God
makes the world is analogous to the way a carpenter makes
a cabinet or a potter makes a pot.

Since analogy is not logical, there is no possible way in
which the Creation myth can be made into a factual statement. Properly understood, "God made the world" is
neither a scientific explanation of the origin of the universe
nor a philosophical answer to the ontological question of
being, for each of these demand some sort of factual state-

ment. It is instead an assertion that is "fundamentally concerned to give a positive answer to the baffling mystery of the meaning of our life here and now as finite, transient creatures."[3] It is meant to give us ultimate security in the face of existential problems of guilt, futility, and estrangement; and it accomplishes this by asserting that "earth" has connections with and dependence on a higher order of permanence and perfection known as "heaven." No matter what life may bring, God is supreme, his love is unyielding, his power infinite, for he made us. Creation, then, establishes a meaningful relationship between man and the divine; as Paul Tillich put it, "the word 'creation' is one of the great symbol-words describing the relation of God to the universe."[4]

Enlightened theology, particularly since Aquinas, has understood the analogical nature of Creation, that is, that God *created* the world in a manner analogous to the way a potter *creates* a pot. However, only the verb "create" has been seen as analogical; the separation between "Creator" and "creation," deriving from the separation of solids, has been taken as fact. But this separation is no less analogical than the verb itself, since the split-level universe with "Creator" at the top and "creation" below is built on the analogy of the political hierarchy. Theology is therefore in the curious position of asserting analogical relationships as doctrine, as historical or factual truths. This, of course, is just one more way in which that reality which is beyond explanation, thought, and words—the no-thing behind all things—is turned into a mere "thing," albeit a Superthing. As such, this reality enters the objective realm of science and is ripe for systematic examination and refutation.

The "otherness" of God is therefore analogical, and founded on the grammatical logic of solids inherent in the noun. But this "otherness" forms one of the basic assumptions about the structure of reality—an assumption that is jealously guarded by theology. Thus God is described as infinitely removed from his creation, beyond the logical rules of the earthly order, so completely apart that he must "reveal" himself in specific acts. His "otherness" has become his "hiddenness" and his incursions have become "miracles." Hence the recurrent call for "signs" of God's power. In the Gospels, great emphasis is laid on the virgin birth, the open tomb, raising from the dead, and the healing of leprosy and blindness. Miracle healings and glossolalia are still with us. Thus, every attempt to destroy the "otherness" of God is condemned: to find God in the world is heresy; to find him in man is blasphemy. Yet the separation of "Creator" and "creation" is simply the extension of the grammatical qualities of the noun into a metaphysical dualism and a theological doctrine.

The most thoroughgoing attempt in Christian theology to preserve the analogical separation of "Creator" and "creation" as logical fact is the doctrine of creation *ex nihilo,* creation "out of nothing." First appearing at the hands of Theophilus of Antioch (ca. A.D. 180), it was later elaborated by Tertullian (A.D. 160–240) as a defense against Gnostic dualism. According to the defenders of creation out of nothing, a creation out of *something* would mean that the "something" was either made by another god or was itself eternal. This leaves us with either two gods or a dualism of God and some kind of stuff which, being eternal, is another god. Both of these absolute dualisms are rejected by the assertion of creation out of *nothing,* which makes God the ultimate and only source of the "stuff" of creation. The creation is therefore subordinate *to,* rather than eternal *with,* God.

This doctrine was also an answer to monistic naturalism,

which asserts that God either makes the universe "out of himself" or is himself synonymous with it. By denying the infinite separation of "Creator" and "creation," monism either destroys God or turns him into a devil. On the one hand, if God is synonymous with the universe, the term "God" is, in Tillich's phrase, "semantically superfluous."[5] On the other hand, if God made the universe out of himself, then *he* is the source of evil—and therefore a devil. To escape from attributing evil to God we must say that evil is the absence of good (after Augustine) or an illusion —somewhat like the Hindu idea of the world as *maya*— which softens the accusation but does not remove the difficulty. God becomes the Great Deceiver. Both of these monisms are rejected by maintaining the separation of "Creator" and "creation" implied in the idea of creation out of nothing.

Now surely it is clear that this doctrine is fraught with utter nonsense. Firstly, by attempting to avoid dualism the doctrine falls into monism, for the one God existing prior to the act of Creation is fully monistic. And, if we refuse to talk of God *prior to* Creation, asserting that God as Creator is known only *after* Creation, we make God dependent on the universe, which surely destroys him as the Absolute. God becomes part of a Creator/creation unity that is dangerously close to monism. Secondly, by attempting to avoid monism, the doctrine leaves us with a dualism of God and Evil, for Evil exists but was not "created" by God. But, logically, if God *did* create out of nothing, then the appearance of Evil must also be attributed to him. Indeed, God is fully responsible for Evil—whether we call it man's sin, Satan's wickedness, or the operation of blind chance—for God allowed men to sin, created Satan, and established the laws of chance. Moreover, as Omniscience, he *knew* it! He is therefore the accomplice of Evil. Now there is nothing wrong with dualism or monism, if one is philosophically disposed toward one of these views. The point is that, as protection against dualism and monism, the doctrine of creation out of nothing is a total failure.

Nor is this the end of such difficulties. If the separation of "Creator" and "creation" is maintained not as analogy but as fact, the creation is separated from its divine ground and God is made into a "thing" that can be separated. This implies that the creation can exist independent of the Creator, which makes him unnecessary. Furthermore, by separating God in time—as prior to the world—we turn him into a creature of time. And, as Alan Watts points out, "the moment you bring God into space and time, there is neither time nor space for anything else."[6] Creation "out of nothing," moreover, becomes a statement about the "origin" of the universe: an event *before* which there was "nothing" and *after* which there was a universe. Science, as noted, finds this to be irresponsible, unverifiable, and meaningless, an illegitimate theory in the realm of "fact."

To maintain the separation of "Creator" and "creation" is therefore to bring myth into the realm of "things" and "events"—nouns and verbs—and therefore subject to the test of logic. Thus, if God was everything there was before creation, it is impossible to be sure if he is God at all. With only God existing, the word "God" becomes meaningless, for it excludes nothing and is therefore without definition. We might just as well label "God" as "everything" or "nothing" or "blub," for the naming of an indefinable is completely arbitrary. The separation of "Creator" and "creation" leads, therefore, to a series of double binds and automatic refutations. Turning analogy into logic leads to systematic contradiction. There is simply no way to build a systematic theology on analogical statements, for the linguistic elements themselves are analogical. Creation must be accepted *as myth*—that is, as analogy—or not at all.

Traditional theological doctrines are primarily built on metaphorical and analogical statements—taken as fact. Theology, therefore, is a systematic extension of the metaphysic of language. This is perhaps most clearly seen in the so-called arguments for the existence of God. The Argument from Design made popular by William Paley in his *Natural Philosophy* (1802) sees the universe as a "design," which must, therefore, imply a "Designer." What is this but the logic of grammar? The well-known Causal Argument sees the universe as an "effect," which inevitably implies a "cause"—God. Like the Argument from Design, this argument rests on the primary subject-object "logic" of Indo-European grammar. The Ontological Argument for God's existence, first put forth by Anselm (1033–1109), argues that since we have a concept of a Perfect Being in our minds, such a Being must necessarily exist. If he did not exist, he would not be perfect, for we could then conceive of a *more* perfect being who did exist. In essence, the Ontological Argument aims at filling a grammatical slot in our grammar corresponding to the concept of "a Being." The fact that "perfection" is said to include "existence" is the result of Bergson's "logic of solids"—the extension of the existence of concrete things to the realm of abstract things. It would seem, then, that any metaphysical argument for God's existence that works within the framework of logic and words can do little more than argue from its own grammatical logic.

Yet even supposing for a moment that the assertion "God made the world" is logical and factual, what is its importance? What does it mean? What language game are we playing? On the one hand, it may seem intellectually satisfying for some, but only if one fails to ask the next *logical* question, "Who or what made God?" Moreover, God-the-Creator is God defined by *what he does:* "God" is "he-who-created-the-world"—in which case our statement, "God made the world," means simply "he-who-created-the-world created the world." If we assume, then, that our language game is one of making logical statements, we are sorely mistaken. Our "God" is in fact a filler for a gap in our knowledge, and the gap has been produced by grammar. Grammatical logic posits that the noun "creation" requires another noun, "Creator"; by this logic we drum up an apparent hole in our knowledge which we then plug up with "God."

On the other hand, since the "Creator" is defined by his "creation," there is considerable evidence for calling him not "God" but "Satan." A glance at the daily newspaper reveals a daily resurrection of Dante's Inferno: gangland warfare, teen-age terrorism in American streets, mass beatings and bombings and burnings in a dozen crisis zones around the world. If God is absolutely "good," he has apparently abandoned man to a world that is much like a giant machine full of undiscovered horrors, which is slowly growing rusty at the joints, running down, and grinding humanity to bits.

Unless modern man can learn to be satisfied with metaphorical and mythical theology—and there is little evidence that he can—the fundamental requirement is a new theological language. And since the problems of theology result from "things" and "events" in the formulas (the nouns and the verbs), a new theological language will necessarily be without both. Moreover, since the Indo-European sentence pattern contains a metaphysic of agent-action, cause-effect, subject-object, which imposes unjustifiable distinctions on theological formulations, a new theological language must avoid this familiar sentence structure.

The language of the Hopi Indians fulfills all of these criteria. An utterance in Hopi is never "logical" in the Aristotelian sense, for Hopi is unable to deliver a propositional statement that predicates some action to an agent. Hopi utterances are all verb-al, and its verbs are all placed in present time. Grammar thus constrains the Hopi to talk of every-thing and every-event as a "happening," a "going-on," a process in the here and now.

Thus, if the traditional statement, "the Creator created the creation," were recast in the structure of the Hopi tongue, the result would be a single utterance in place of a propositional statement, an utterance that would describe creation as a"happening." The English grammatical structure that duplicates this Hopi structure is the single word CREATING.

The -ing verb, such as "creating," is usually taken to be a present tense verb, but is, in fact, tenseless, since it can function as a progressive element in past, present, or future tenses (he was creating, is creating, will be creating). This tenseless (timeless) quality suggests that this grammatical form is ideally suited for assertions about that reality which cannot be "timed"—the eternal now. From the standpoint of Noam Chomsky's transformational grammar, "Creator" and "creation" are nominalizations formed from a basic "kernel," *create*. Thus, "the Creat-or creat-ed the creat-ion" is really redundant, consisting of three variations of a kernel idea. The implication is, of course, that "Creator" is an agentive nominalization.

"Creating" is, in traditional grammar, a gerund and a participle, which means it can function as a verbal noun or as an adjective (creating is fun, a creating process). The peculiar cluster of ideas evoked by this class of word has never been systematically explored by philosophy or theology: tough-minded thinkers have more often avoided processive language and stressed nouns or nominalizations. (Even the father of process philosophy, Whitehead, fell into this pattern with terms such as "occasion," "prehension," "creativity," "lure," "nexus," etc.) It is no surprise, then, that a *language of process based on a processive metaphysic* has never been developed. Nevertheless, the powerfully descriptive and rhythmic qualities of the -ing words have long been recognized and exploited in poetry. Thus, although Whorf's Hopi Indians provide an example of a whole language on this basis, it is not necessary to go beyond an already existing structure within the Indo-European metaphysic, a structure generally overshadowed by the more dominant, noun-verb pattern of the propositional statement.

A description of the "creating" universe emphasizes the whole marvelous process of "creative advance"[7] rather than static completion. The universe is not a finished "creation"; no end point has been reached. It is more a process than a product, so that we may say it is "creating" just as we say it is "evolving" and "developing." These concepts are constantly applied to the formation of galaxies, the rise of life, or the emergence of mind; yet we feel no compulsion to ask, "Who is the Developer, who the Evolver?" Evolution is never seen as an end product, which would imply a Producer, but rather as ongoing process. What we are advocating is an understanding of "creating" as process with no attempt to differentiate it into a cause (Creator) or final effect (creation). Understood this way, the whole idea of "creating" becomes a poetically moving description of virtually every kind of creative change and dynamic movement perceived. As an eminent marine biol-

ogist, Norman Berrill, has put it, "nature, in the intimate
and in the vast is not designed. It is designing. Our own
nature confirms it."[8] And again, "I come again and again
to realize that the process itself is the reality, that creation
is creating, whether it be writing a letter, caring for a child,
or any other piece of living."[9]

Thus far it may seem that we have stressed a view of
creation foreign to Biblical religion. On the contrary, the
ongoing "creating" activity was stressed in Hebrew times
far more than creation as an "event" in the beginning. The
latter idea, however, gets the most attention because it
comes on the first page. The real Maker of the Old Testament, as understood by the prophets centuries before the
Genesis account was written, was the Maker of history,
whose work was visible in the "creating" activity of nature.

> Thou makest springs gush forth in the valleys;
>   they flow between the hills,
> they give drink to every beast of the field;
>   the wild asses quench their thirst. . . .
> From thy lofty abode thou waterest the mountains;
>   the earth is satisfied with the fruit of thy work.
> Thou dost cause the grass to grow for the cattle,
>   and plants for man to cultivate. . . .
> When thou sendest forth thy Spirit, they are created;
>   and thou renewest the face of the ground.
>   (Ps. 104:10–11, 13–14a, 30.)

Surely these words radiate the highest vision of God's
"creating" power to be found in the Bible. Since, however,
the writer's view of the universe was hierarchical, directed
by the King of Kings at the top, it was inevitable that he
would see the power behind "creating" as personal. But
what must be emphasized is that the God who is named is

not God at all—that the genuine mystery of ongoing creation is best preserved by a description of that "creating,"
with no attempt to explain it.

The conception of creation as an "event" in the beginning was, it turns out, an afterthought. Studies of Old
Testament materials have shown that the Genesis account
was written about the time of Deutero-Isaiah (Isa., chs. 40
to 55), during the Babylonian captivity (587–536 B.C.),
which accounts for the extensive parallels between the
Biblical and Babylonian accounts.[10] Scholars now conclude that the Genesis account was written from the perspective of the exodus of the thirteenth century, the most
important event in the religious life of the Hebrews.

The primary point in the Genesis account is that God
produced light out of darkness and order out of chaos.
Before the creative word of God went forth, "the earth was
without form and void, and darkness was upon the face of
the deep" (Gen. 1:2). The Hebrew word *těhôm* (the
deep) is parallel to the Babylonian *Tiamât,* the primeval
monster of Chaos that was slain by the god Marduk at the
foundation of the world. Darkness on the face of *Tiamât*
at his defeat has become, in the Hebrew account, "darkness on the face of the *deep.*" This Creation story, written
some seven centuries *after* Moses' time, was put forth in
the imagery and symbolic motifs of the exodus. At the
beginning of Hebrew history Chaos ruled in the land of
darkness called Egypt, where the Israelites were "nothing"
—a band of slaves. When Moses had to demonstrate his
power before the Pharaoh, he followed the command of
God: "When Pharaoh says to you, 'Prove yourselves by
working a miracle,' then you shall say to Aaron, 'Take
your rod and cast it down before Pharaoh, that it may
become a serpent'" (Ex. 7:9). "Serpent" is *tannîn,* the
mythical monster of Chaos, who lived in the waters of

darkness. By this act Moses demonstrated his power over Chaos and Darkness, and hence the power of his God over the primal deep. Whether *tannîn* is regarded as a "serpent," a mythical monster akin to *Tiamât,* or simply *tĕhôm,* the deep, the message to Pharaoh was unmistakable. Despite further displays by the Pharaoh of Egyptian strength, the exodus finally took place under him who commanded even Chaos—Moses himself.

The exodus was the creation of the Hebrew nation "out of nothing"—out of a band of slaves in the land of darkness, ruled over by the Pharaoh who was later identified as the Dragon, the monster of Chaos. This exodus, involving the creation of light and order out of darkness, the emergence of a nation from the primal waters of the Red Sea, and the destruction of the armies of the Egyptian Dragon, laid down the pattern for a Creation story extending to the whole cosmos. Creation was first, then, a "creating" in the actual life of the Hebrews, a manifestation of activity in their midst. Their God was he who performed miracles in the Sinai desert, going before them "by day in a pillar of cloud . . . by night in a pillar of fire" (Ex. 13:21) and slaying their enemies at the battle of Jericho and after. Creation as "creating" was seen and understood by Hebrew poets long before creation as an "event" in the beginning. Once "creating" became an "event," it became a pseudoscientific account of the "origins," and demanded a separation of the "Creator" as some-thing prior to and "above" the "creating" process: the logic of solids.

It may be objected by some that we are rejecting the beauty and richness of traditional Christianity by treating its symbolism and mythology this way. On the contrary, we are trying to reveal the thought structures underlying these modes of thinking, since modern man is no longer able to interpret them mythically. Properly understood, symbol and myth are profound ways of dealing with religious truth. Religious experience is the confrontation of a reality transcending time and space, and therefore words. The world of the spaceless and timeless is only communicable metaphorically and analogically—that is, in terms of space and time. Symbols are therefore pictures of the nonspatial, and myths are temporal narratives of the nontemporal. In short, symbols are images of the unimaginable and myths are tales of the untellable. Myth and symbol therefore describe the indescribable by bringing it "down" from the realm of the wordless to the common level of words. The result is that mythical language is continually confused with factual and historical language. As fact, it is rightly rejected by many as nonsense, and reduced to "mere" mythology. Thus, if the reality behind the words is our real concern—and it *must* be if theology is to carry on in a responsible fashion—then a language structure that approaches this reality in the thought forms of our day must be our goal.

The theology of the "creating" universe is therefore theology without symbolism and mythology. By adopting a totally different linguistic structure, it moves to a new point of view from which symbolism and mythology are no longer possible or necessary. Without spatial nouns and temporal verbs such a theology is incapable of the idolatrous worship of words; it is incapable of making distinctions that issue in the hypothetical existence of the "transcendent"; and it studiously avoids founding religious truth on historical events. Dualism disappears, supernatural beings disappear, invisible realms disappear—along with the incredulous denial of secular man. The theology of the "creating" universe asserts nothing that could possibly deny God; it simply recognizes the impossibility of asserting God in any meaningful way. Nor does it assert anything that can possibly clash with science. Described as "creating," this universe is not explained, categorized, pigeonholed, or "leveled" into absent spirit and dead matter. Instead, it is asserted to be *pro-ducing,* "leading forward" the new, the different, the incredible, even as we watch. This is the theology of experience.

Linguistic analysts and logical positivists have long known that theological statements were immune to both disproof and verification. While the truth could never be known, it was a matter of personal choice whether one accepted or rejected the reality of God. But the theology of the "creating" universe not only dissolves the duality of "creator" and "creation"; it also dissolves the duality of the faith that accepts and the doubt that rejects. Moving to a new conceptual position, we find it impossible and irrelevant to think of "ultimate" reality as something "beyond" which can therefore be accepted or rejected. Instead, the new position grounds reality in the sheer immediacy of the world we experience, the "creating" world, which is *here,* beyond belief. This is surely what Paul meant when he wrote: "All that may be known of God by men lies plain before their eyes. . . . His invisible attributes . . . have been visible, ever since the world began, to the eye of reason, in the things he has made." (Rom. 1:19–20, NEB.)

The "creating" universe is a unity of man, God, and nature within a single harmonious process. As such it is similar to the world of preliterate man, where everything was alive, where man was one with the animals and trees, and the forces of the universe flowed through all things. It is probably impossible for us to duplicate this world view today. Nevertheless, the concept of "creating" has many features in common with the primitive concept of *mana.*

The Polynesian term *mana* was first pointed out by R. H.

Codrington in *The Melanesians: Studies in Their Anthropology and Folk-Lore* (1891). Since then an almost identical concept has been found in the Algonquin Indian term *manitou,* the Sioux Indian *wakanda,* the Iroquois *orenda,* and the *mulunga* of the African Bantu tribe.[11] These terms are not easily translated into Indo-European languages. *Mana,* for example, is a kind of supernatural power, though it is not *super*natural but instead permeates the whole of the natural world. Nor is it personal. As Ernst Cassirer has pointed out:

> This conception is still quite indifferent, one might say "neutral," to a host of distinctions which our theoretical view of being and happening and our advanced religious feeling would apply to it . . . . The more one tries to "determine" it, i.e., to interpret it in the categories of distinctions and contradictions familiar to our thinking, the more widely one misses its true nature.[12]

Consequently, attempts to translate these terms into Indo-European languages are fraught with difficulty. *Mana* has often been translated "spirit," and ill-informed missionaries often translated the Indian terms *manitou* and *wakanda* as "Great Spirit," leading them to assume the Indians had a conception of a supernatural Being. Such a translation (into an English noun) reifies the meaning and misses it altogether. Properly understood, *mana, manitou, wakanda, orenda,* and *mulunga* do not fit into the categories of noun, verb, adjective, or adverb—yet may be used as all of these. Cassirer points out that these terms can be variously translated as "remarkable, very strong, very great, very old, strong in magic, wise in magic, supernatural, divine—or in a substantive sense as power, magic, sorcery, fortune, success, godhead, delight."[13] The closest English word, Cassirer suggests, is "mystery," though it is neither as limited nor as definite as our concept of mystery. Moreover, it must be "mystery" understood as adjectival, verbal, adverbial, and substantive. Above all, *mana* and its kindred terms do not denote anything conceptual but instead suggest a certain impression. These terms, then, most often appear as interjections or exclamations in the face of anything unusual, wonderful, terrifying, or mysterious.

Now the word "creating," as already noted, is at once nominal, adjectival, and verbal. It is, therefore, like *mana*, for it is "indifferent" or "neutral" to the distinctions of clear-cut nouns, adjectives, and verbs. "Creating" does not imply an underlying substance; it does not denote a definable quality; it does not describe an easily conceptualized action. It is neither a "thing" nor an "event." Indeed, "creating" means something new in every new situation. The usual conceptualized form of "create" as "make"— the potter making the pot—is too limited, for "creating" means evolving, growing, moving, changing, with the attendant qualities of surprise and mystery. The "creating" universe is all of this: continual growth and change, with a surprise at every turn and a mystery enveloping the whole.

To point to the similarity between "creating" and *mana* is not to advocate primitive animism in place of modern theology, nor is it to recommend these primitive terms as valuable currency today. The point is, rather, that the ultimate mystery of this world is little more understood today than it was in prehistoric times. The ongoing "creating" process—though it has been pursued into the stars on the one hand and into the atom on the other—is so marvelous and terrifying that we can do little more than exclaim with the native of the magical forest, *"Wakanda"*— it is "creating." The divisive structures of symbolism and myth have in some respects taken away from this mystery, if only by challenging modern credibility. And, in terms of capturing the sheer wonder of existence and in terms of evoking the deepest reverence in the mind of man, these structures are no improvement on the unconceptualized feelings evoked by a vision of the "creating" universe.

The "creating" universe is the world seen in "the nick of time," the timeless moment of actual experiencing. It has meaning for man, who finds himself part of it and it of him, in a way that the doctrine of Creation can never have. And if "creation" is, as Paul Tillich suggests, one of the great symbol words describing God's relation to the universe, "creating" is that too, though it replaces metaphor with a description and finds divinity as a Beyond Within. "Creating" is therefore what the universe does, what man does, and what "God" does, though all this "doing" is one doing. "Creating" is not the external manipulation of matter to make a "thing," as in modern technology, but the working out of a power that is within. "Creating" is thus synonymous with *pro-ducing* (leading forth), *e-volving* (turning outward), and *de-veloping* (unfolding), as when the growing bud of a plant turns outward, unfolds, and leads itself forth as a flower from within. Indeed, the idea of the "creating" universe as *growing* from within is exactly what "creating" means, for "create" derives ultimately from the Indo-European base *kerē* meaning "grow" or "bring forth."

A theological description of the "creating" universe thus turns out to be fully scientific, for the biologist watching the amazing activity of microbes and algae, the astronomer tuning in on wheeling galaxies and exploding stars, and the chemist discovering the potential of patterned star dust—all are drawn by the irresistible magic of a world that is "creating." There is no need to believe or doubt, for this is beyond belief and unbelief. "Creating" is found in the midst of life, in the struggling first thoughts of a child, in the flying fingers of the concert pianist, in the loops and twirls of Olympic skaters, in poetry and painting and sculpturing, in the fantastic inventions of man that are pouring out to the world almost every hour, and in the silent majesty of the rising moon and the hanging stars. All is endless pattern, the continual "mattering" of energy, the unbelievable harmony of hydrogen, hanging in the blackness of space like a cascade of sparks in the night.

6

The Incarnating Christ

Christianity is Christ. From the time of the first proclamation of the gospel, the center of Christian worship and belief has been "Jesus of Nazareth, a man attested to you by God with mighty works and wonders and signs which God did through him in your midst, as you yourselves know" (Acts 2:22). This man, whose words and deeds burn across the centuries, who came in the fullness of time, lived and died to save men from sin, has become known as the Son of God, Redeemer of humanity, Prince of Peace, Savior of the world. Standing at the hinge of history, where time reverses itself, this man has become the center of much of Western art, the man most talked about, most read about, most written about. The most controversial figure in human history, this man is literally on the lips of infants from end to end of Christendom. It is inevitable, then, that he form the center of any theology.

Throughout the New Testament, Jesus is the focus. He is the man wearing a crown of thorns, and the divine Son at the right hand of God in the heavenly city of the Apocalypse. He is the friend of sinners and the veneration of saints. He is the infant in the cradle and the man on the cross, forgiving those we scorn, teaching those who despise him, raising those who are dead. A star rises over his birthplace, the sea stands still at his command, the dead rise from their graves at his death. And after it all, he walks through history in risen glory, victorious over sin and death. The object of worship, he is the stumbling block for historians and the point where human thought crashes against the unknown. For Christians he is, in some sense, divine—or God himself.

It is not surprising that we are confused. There is ample evidence that those who had firsthand experience of Jesus were also confused, unable to comprehend his teaching and personality. After the crucifixion, the disciples went through severe depression, utter loss of hope, and a complete disintegration of community spirit. The dramatic realization of what and who Jesus was came days or weeks later. Only with hindsight, and with the profound experience of Easter grasping their whole being were they able to begin to comprehend the man with whom they had lived and traveled for over thirty months. Yet once this *was* grasped, life could never be the same again. In Paul's words, "From now on, therefore, we regard no one from a human point of view; even though we once regarded Christ from a human point of view, we regard him thus no longer." (II Cor. 5:16.)

In dealing with this man at the heart of Christianity, we run up against the old problem, the danger of reducing the unspeakable to mere words. The necessary approach must be simply to "observe and describe," refusing to hammer mystery into logical and factual creeds. For theologians have said things of Jesus that he would not have them say and fitted him into categories that are their own, not his. This began with those who were there, the Jewish people who had long awaited the coming of the Christ, the Messiah who would lead men into the New Age. Yet Jesus himself, unwilling to accept its political overtones, was hesitant about the title "Christ." The same is true of the title "Son of God." In Hebrew thinking, "Son of God" carried connotations of kingship and divine calling; in Greek religion it had reference to numerous semidivine heroes sprung from the union of a mortal with an immortal god: Perseus, Hercules, Theseus, Jason, Helen of Troy. Jesus was again reluctant to assume this title, although Matthew and Luke later provided a mythical birth story in which Jesus sprang from the union of the mortal Mary and the immortal Spirit of God. And finally, Jesus resisted the title "Son of Man" because of its supernatural connotations (Mark 8:38; 14:62) deriving from the Old Testament (Dan. 7:13).

The most incredible title applied to Jesus was "Lord" (*kyrios*) and it shattered the Old Testament concept of God. The word "Lord" was accepted not only by the Hebrews as the name of God but also by the Greeks and Romans as the title for the absolute ruler of the Empire, who had divine authority. This was why the Jews could not accept the "Lordship" of the Emperor, for their allegiance was to their own Lord, Jesus. And it was this title which was universally accepted, by Jesus and by Christians ever since. In Paul's words, "God has highly exalted him and bestowed on him the name which is above every name, that at the name of Jesus every knee should bow, in heaven and on earth and under the earth, and every tongue confess that Jesus Christ is Lord." (Phil. 2:9–11.)

As noted earlier, there is no logical way to link "heaven" and "earth." The only linguistic devices available are metaphor and analogy. In the cosmology of the New Testament, the assertion that Jesus *is* Lord is a metaphorical assertion of identity between the divine and human realms, in the one man in whom "all things are held together" (Col. 1:17, NEB). This understanding of "Lord" quite literally smashed the dichotomy between this world and the divine realm "above." In adopting this title, Jesus issued a challenge to the prevailing idea of the distant God, the absent God. "The kingdom of God," he said, "is within you." (Luke 17:21, KJV.) Yet the history of theology is a history of retaining the *super*natural God despite the fact that Jesus brought him into the midst of this world.

Alongside the metaphorical identity of Jesus as Lord there are at least three other explanations in the Bible of the person of Jesus. The first, chronologically, was the assertion by Paul that "God was in Christ reconciling the world to himself" (II Cor. 5:19), an assertion that turns the metaphorical identity into a kind of logical proposition that *explains* the identity. And to say that "God was in Christ" is certainly not the same as saying "Jesus *is* Lord." The second explanation occurs in the Gospels of Matthew and Luke, written some forty years after the Easter event. Pressured perhaps by the necessity of proving Jesus' uniqueness, and confronted with a roster of divine heroes in Greek religion, these Gospelists developed a mythology in which Jesus had been born of a woman "visited" by the Spirit. Apart from Greek parallels, this myth indicates an attempt to make Jesus the fulfillment of Old Testament prophecy. But, like the Creation myth, the myth of Jesus' paranormal birth rests on the cosmology of two realms, "heaven" and "earth," the latter of which has been visited by the Spirit from the former.

The third explanation occurs in the Gospel of John, written around A.D. 100. John's account is highly metaphysical but preserves the dualism of the other explanations: "In the beginning was the Word, and the Word was with God, and the Word was God . . . . And the Word became flesh and dwelt among us." (John 1:1, 14.) The "Word" is a direct borrowing from the Greek concept of

logos, a philosophical concept tracing through the Stoics to
Heraclitus, meaning that creative and generative force
which was understood as in some sense divine. The Jewish
philosopher Philo, in attempting to make the Hebrew Yahweh philosophically respectable, had borrowed the idea of
the logos and linked it with the dynamic principle of the
universe, the power by which the Creator works and by
which he reveals himself to the world. John in turn borrowed Philo's idea and made the logos into the Word
through whom "all things were made" (John 1:3), and
Jesus became the Word made flesh.

In developing the doctrine of the incarnation, the church
fathers failed to grasp the nature of metaphorical language. Had they grasped this, they might have seen that
"Jesus Christ *is* Lord" is similar to the assertions that
Jesus *is* the Lamb of God, the Bread of Life, or the True
Vine. One does not erect a metaphysics upon metaphor.
But these early theologians instead proceeded to develop a
logical formulation of the incarnation based on the dualistic premise of a split-level universe. They failed to see
that the dualism of "divine" and "human" was an analogy
with the political state and that the separation between
"Word" and "flesh" was the "logic of solids," that is, the
logic of a noun-oriented language. They therefore concentrated their attention on explaining how the "divine" and
"human" were united in Jesus.

The story of the development of the incarnation doctrine is a long and complicated one, involving numerous
attempts that were dismissed as heretical. The church
fathers somehow had to justify the worship of Jesus that
had grown up in early Christian communities. At the same
time, in making God one with Jesus, they had to resolve
the apparent problem that God had died on the cross. Yet
to deny that the union was total would be to turn the whole

salvation into a playacting manipulated by God. Every
solution was tried, including the idea that a substitute had
died on the cross and the notion that Jesus had been taken
down before death. But ultimately a solution was reached
by the introduction of the Greek concept of *hypostasis*
("substance," usually translated "person"). The key to
the success of the Chalcedon formulation lies in the assertion that Jesus had two "natures" in one "person":

> One and the same Christ, . . . recognized in TWO
> NATURES, WITHOUT CONFUSION, WITHOUT CHANGE,
> WITHOUT DIVISION, WITHOUT SEPARATION; the dis-
> tinction of natures being in no way annulled by the
> union, but rather the characteristics of each nature
> being preserved and coming together to form one
> person and substance (*hypostasis*), not as parted or
> separated into two persons, but one and the same
> Son and Only-begotten God the Word, Lord Jesus
> Christ.[1]

Paul Tillich has noted that "it is unfair to criticize the
Church Fathers for their use of Greek concepts. There
were no other available conceptual expressions of man's
cognitive encounter with his world."[2] Nevertheless, if the
Chalcedon formula seems strange today, it is probably
due to the strange equation of "person" and "substance"
—an equation that has no bite in modern thinking.

Tillich has again noted that "the christological dogma
saved the church, but with very inadequate conceptual
tools."[3] If the Chalcedon formula is taken as a solution
within its mythological framework of supernaturalism, it
represents perhaps the best possible attempt to preserve
the mystery of the person of Jesus. Nevertheless, it focuses
our attention on the one crucial point on which the doctrine stands or falls: should Christ be understood—should
anything in Christianity be understood—in terms of super-

naturalism? For christological formulas built on super-naturalism attempt to relate logically two different "realms" that can only be related symbolically, by metaphor and analogy.

Indo-European languages, as emphasized earlier, are grounded in the spatial distinctions of the noun. Since nouns define differences and overlook relationships, the whole mythical scheme of the incarnation is steeped in what seem to be unreal distinctions and artificially constructed relationships. Thus Mary, the mother of Jesus, is "visited" by the Spirit, and Jesus is the son "sent" from "on high." The Spirit "descends" on him from "above" at his baptism, and he is continually addressing his words to his Father "in heaven." In the complementary myth of the ascension, in which the risen Jesus "goes back" to his place "in heaven," he is literally "lifted up" to take his place at the right hand of God. All this has left theology with a mountain of purely mechanical problems: How does God "get a message through" from his world to us? How does God "bridge the gap" between the divine and human to make his "entry" into history? Once he has "broken through," what is the mode of union of the divine Word with the human flesh? How does the Word "get back" from "this world" to the other realm "out there"?

Once again the conclusion is inevitable: theology is based on the distinctions of mythology and symbolism, which are in turn founded on the metaphysic of the Indo-European languages in which they are expressed. Just as dualistic language leads us to conclude a "Creator" behind "creation," it leads us to conclude there must be a "Father" behind the "Son," the "Word" behind the "flesh," "divinity" behind "Jesus." By the time of the patristic councils the supernaturalistic world view was so deeply entrenched in Greek and Hebrew thinking that it

was certain Jesus would be seen within its framework.
Nevertheless, a careful look at the record reveals the inherent fallacy. The evidence to be used in a doctrine of
Christ is not a rigid *idea* of an unchanging, separate God,
but the actual, visible evidence (Observe and describe!)
that Jesus was beaten, was crucified, and died on the
cross. Nothing is known about "God" apart from what is
revealed before our eyes, and that revelation must be seen
with a clarity that cuts through all preconceptions of *what*
is being revealed. In grammatical terms, we do not have a
"revelation" that necessitates a "Revealer": we have a
visible process of REVEALING.

Perhaps the most forceful statement of this principle is
that set down by William Hamilton:

> Let us assume you are asked, "Do you believe in the
> divinity of Christ?" It makes no difference whether
> the questioner is impeccably orthodox and suspects
> that you are not, or wildly unitarian and suspects you
> of dogmatism. The question implies a comparison
> between two clearly known categories: one, called
> the divine or divinity; the other, the man Jesus. And
> the questioner wishes to know whether or not you
> find these two known categories commensurable. But
> the point is this: we do not have two *known* cate-
> gories at all. We have Jesus the man. . . . We do not
> *know* any separate category of divinity, a separate
> divine essence by means of which we can define
> Jesus.[4]

This is the crucial fact that theologians must grasp. We
know nothing of a Creator; we have only the world.
We know nothing of heaven; we have only the universe. We
know nothing of the Word; we have only Jesus. We have
no explanations; we can only describe. The point about
Jesus is that he stands—as does every man—enshrouded
in mystery, just as the whole universe is overflowing with

unutterable mystery. By seeking to ex-plain, we "flatten
out" the mystery, but by describing we may let the wonder
of it live on.

Perhaps the thorniest problem connected with the incarnation is its meaning as an "event" in history. Jesus
was a historical person who lived at a specific time in the
past; therefore, whatever happened is primarily describable
in historical terms. Yet, if the incarnation refers simply to
an event in history, and if this means that the redemption
of man throughout the total stream of history was accomplished by this single event, then there are a host of
insolubles. For, if God's action is confined to an event, if
it does not rise above this event, then God's redemptive act
is merely one act among many. In what way is *this* event
more important than any other—say the poisoning of
Socrates, or the hanging of Dietrich Bonhoeffer? Moreover, supposing for the moment that the incarnation does
somehow rise above all other events, how in fact does it
affect the rest of history? How does the incarnation event
change things? How does it redeem men? Men living hundreds of years after—or before—Jesus? For "history" is
not something linear, like an electric wire along which there
flows a current in both directions if contact is made at a
single point. Yet, even apart from such problems, there are
real dangers in making the incarnation entirely into a
datable event—the same dangers that lie in the idea of
Creation as an event "in the beginning." For Christianity is
left wide open for the deistic suggestion that that event was
the last; that God has since withdrawn, ceased to act, and
is perhaps dead. Moreover, some will go on to add that we
have misinterpreted that one event, that Jesus was "merely"
a man and that no divine act *ever* occurred.

The incarnation, however, rises above the temporal
when it becomes not a historical truth about the man Jesus,

but an eternal—that is, a timeless—truth about Christ. Jesus was born and died as a man, but Christ is that timeless "creating" Word who was with God in the beginning and who sits with God until the end. And, it is precisely because such myths have accumulated around the incarnation that we know it is a timeless truth—a tale of the untellable, an image of the unimaginable, a story not of "what happened" but of "what happens." As such it is a truth told in "the nick of time," the present moment.

The traditional statements of the incarnation all rest on the Indo-European dualism of "heaven" and "earth." These formulations break down into three basic parts, which correspond to the parts of a propositional sentence: subject-verb-object. There is first of all the historical event of the past, which may be designated by the past-tense verb, "incarnated." Secondly, there is the visible manifestation of this event, Jesus of Nazareth, which can be designated as an "incarnation." Seen as an effect or object of the event, "incarnation" implies a cause or subject (nonsensical as this may seem), which may be designated "Incarnator." Thus, "the Incarnator incarnated the incarnation." This, in strictly logical terms, is what the doctrine of incarnation means: that God became man. Paul Tillich has labeled this "nonsensical."[5] For there is in fact no evidence for the "subject" of our proposition, "Incarnator"—we have only Jesus the man. Moreover, the real mystery is destroyed by such a lifeless formulation, which throws the whole thing onto the dust heap of history. But, again, in our new language, suggested by Hopi, subjects and objects, "things" and "events" disappear, and we have in their place a dynamic, living description of process in the timeless moment: INCARNATING.

God "incarnating," nature "incarnating," man "incarnating"—all are one in the "incarnating" universe. To understand the meaning of the "incarnating" universe is not only to arrive at the core of Christianity, but also to find oneself at the center of mystical religion. It is to discover that underlying the symbols of Christianity is the universal truth underlying the symbols of all the major religions. Moreover, it is to discover the God of Christianity who smashes the "God" of Christianity—the God who ceases to be "God" in becoming man.

The idea of the "Word" of God goes all the way back to the earliest Hebrew understandings of Creation. In the beginning God made the world by command (Let there be light!); that is, he used *words* to call the universe into being. Thus, the psalmist: "By the word of the Lord the heavens were made, and all their host by the breath of his mouth. . . . For he spoke, and it came to be; he commanded, and it stood forth." (Ps. 33:6, 9.) "He sends forth his command to the earth; his word runs swiftly." (Ps. 147:15.) The Word of God was, therefore, the very "creating" power of God. Thus Paul, in a letter specifically written to guard against narrow interpretations of Christ, categorically linked Christ with the creating Word of God: "He is the image of the invisible God, the first-born of all creation; for in him all things were created, in heaven and on earth. . . . All things were created through him and for him." (Col. 1:15–16.) And again: "There is one Lord, Jesus Christ, through whom all things came to be." (I Cor. 8:6, NEB.)

The Gospel of John therefore takes up the coming of Christ as a timeless truth, as the very "creating" of God. The Gospel begins like Genesis: *"In the beginning* was the Word . . . ." But, in retelling Creation, John *redefines* Creation itself *as incarnation.* God ceases to be the distant Creator and becomes instead the "creating" power itself: "the Word *was* God." In that phrase, God becomes *inseparable from his actual "creating" activity,* the Word itself. But John goes on to further define Creation, describing the *way* in which the Word creates all things: "the Word *became* flesh." The "creating" Word thus ceases to be a commandment from a distant Creator and becomes instead the power that creates all things by *becoming* all things. The Old Testament image of the Creator as technologist is completely restructured around the image of the Actor "acting" or the Dancer "dancing." The "creating" power creates the world by "incarnating," that is by BECOMING it, just as an actor creates Hamlet by giving up his former identity and becoming Hamlet, or a dancer creates a dance by dancing, so that, as Yeats says, "How can we know the dancer from the dance?"

The gospel of the incarnation is the "incarnating" universe. But *this* "incarnating" is timeless, rising above a single time or a single man. "Creating" by "incarnating" has been going on from the beginning and is going on *now* —not just in Jesus, not just in Christians, but in all "creating," for the Word "was in the world, and the world was made through him, yet the world knew him not" (John 1:10). Jesus himself was a historical person, but Christ is the timeless principle "revealing" in him, for Christ was precisely that "revealing" activity which men had missed from the beginning—the Presence "incarnating" all things and all men. And, just as an actor ceases to be an "actor" in his "acting," God ceases to be "God" and becomes "flesh"—or "fleshing." There is no God apart from man, apart from the universe. Such a "God" is a figment of imagination, a product of crooked thinking. God apart can only be the distant King, the Giant Tyrant, the great bloodsucking "Hound of Heaven." When this "God" comes into the world he comes slumming. But the God who comes to stay comes in flesh, known only as "incarnating."

This is the gospel of love. Not that God reconciled the world to himself from afar but that "God was in Christ reconciling the world to himself" (II Cor. 5:19). To seek God by climbing to heaven or by praying into the distance, to try to win union with him by good deeds, is to ride the waves in search of water, to hunt in darkness with candles looking for fire. God is here, now, "incarnating," staring us in the eyes, closer to us than we are to ourselves. We can never come "to" God, never escape "from" God, for he is here wherever we go. This is the infinite love that will not let us go. As Paul wrote, "I am convinced that there is nothing in death or life, in the realm of spirits or super-human powers, in the world as it is or the world as it shall be, in the forces of the universe, in heights or depths— nothing in all creation that can separate us from the love of God in Christ Jesus our Lord." (Rom. 8:38–39, NEB.)

The proclamation of the gospel is the proclamation of the redemption wrought by Christ. This means that the "incarnating" universe is a redeemed universe, an under-standing of which returns us again to the myth of the Fall. The Fall of man is brought about by his assertion of pride, the withdrawal into egoism that sets a man off from nature and God. Divided from nature, the matrix of his birth, man no longer sees it as part of himself, nor himself as part of the universal harmony. As a result of man's darkened vision, the universe becomes a split-level world of brute nature and a distant God. Thus, the Fall of man is a cosmic fall—the distorted vision of a broken universe. This is what is meant by the symbolic "thorns and thistles" (Gen. 3:18) sprouting in Eden after the forbidden fruit is eaten. In Milton's *Paradise Lost,* at the moment when Eve puts forth "her rash hand in evil hour," the whole earth feels the wound, nature sighs in woe; and when Adam follows Eve, the earth trembles with pangs and groans, the sky lowers and thunders and weeps sad drops of rain.[6] The Fall of man is the fall of the whole universe, which was what Paul meant when he wrote that "the creation waits with eager longing for the revealing," and that in the redemption "creation itself will be set free from its bondage," for "we know that the whole creation has been groaning in travail together until now; and not only the creation, but we ourselves" (Rom. 8:19, 21-23).

Thus, the longed-for redemption of the prophets was always cosmic redemption, a renewed vision of the whole universe as infinite harmony. These prophetic visions sound strange to modern man unless it be remembered that they are simply a symbolic reversal of man's loss of Eden. Therefore they reveal a cosmic harmony where the division brought on by egoism, and its resultant darkened vision, has disappeared. In this redeemed world, says Isaiah, "the wolf shall dwell with the lamb, and the leopard shall lie down with the kid, and the calf and the lion and the fatling together, and a little child shall lead them" (Isa. 11:6). This is a transformed vision of the world brought on in the fullness of time by God himself, in a covenant that betroths man to God forever (Hos. 2:19). Thus John, setting down his apocalyptic vision, describes "a new heaven and a new earth" (Rev. 21:1) in terms of *the union of all things.* He sees the tree of life standing beside the river of life from Eden, which is flowing "through the middle of the street" (Rev. 22:2). But why the middle of the street? Because the garden has been brought *into the city:* man and nature are at last one. But this is no earthly city, it is a city carried *up to heaven,* the New Jerusalem: man and God are together at last. At the center is God, at his right hand is Christ, and all around are the redeemed. The river of life flows from beneath God's throne, and *heaven* is ablaze with the jewels of the *earth*—jasper, sapphire, emerald, topaz, amethyst, pearl, and gold. And there is no more Temple (Rev. 21:22), for "the dwelling of God is with men" (Rev. 21:3).

Yet this redeemed world was not managed by some miraculous feat of cosmic engineering. It was not and is not accomplished by a dramatic breaking in of God—he is already here. It is instead the moment when the scales fall away from man's eyes. In that moment man suddenly *sees* the "incarnating" universe: he lives "in Christ." And "in Christ, he is a new creation; the old has passed away, behold, the new has come." (II Cor. 5:17.) This new life "in Christ" is life "in the Spirit," for "the Lord is the Spirit" (II Cor. 3:17)—and when we are really "in the Spirit" of things we are in God in whom "we live and move and have our being" (Acts 17:28). In *this* moment, in "the nick of time," eternal life is ours.

To see the universe as "incarnating" is to see a newly created world, the body of Christ—an invisible church smashing the bonds of visible churches. For the "Lord of heaven and earth does not live in shrines made by man" (Acts 17:24). To see this new creation is to see the sacred within the profane. It is, as Blake said,

> To see a World in a grain of sand
> And a Heaven in a wild flower,
> Hold Infinity in the palm of your hand
> And Eternity in an hour.
> —*William Blake,*
> *"Auguries of Innocence."*

To see the universe as "incarnating" turns *ex-istence* (coming out) into *ec-stasy* (standing out), for the cosmos turns into a marvelous dance and rhythm. The "incarnating" universe contains the Mystery of something, we know not what, embodied, the vision of the world as a veil, the tantalizing feeling of something revealed and hidden, seen and not seen, all in one moment. No words can capture this, for to capture it is to destroy it. It cannot be explained, for it is soon explained away, broken down into verbal bits that can only be strung together like cheap beads. Beyond all words is the vision itself, which like the sight of green leaves or the feel of cold water, goes beyond all analysis and definition. This Mystery, which comes through all experience, reduces man to helplessness before the unutterable. No "God" can make sense of it, for nothing can add a cubit to this primal experience of seizing the ragged edge of the universe with the naked hands.

And what of ourselves? If the universe is "incarnating," then we are too. The Word became flesh—*all flesh*. Jesus draws us to himself but only to point us back at ourselves. His greatness is our greatness, for he shows us what we might be. Thus the "incarnating" Word we see in him must be found in ourselves, so that we can exclaim with Paul, "It is no longer I who live, but Christ who lives in me."

And, lest this seem extravagant, there is a parable told by Jesus in which the Son of Man, sitting in heavenly glory, separates mankind into groups as a shepherd might separate the sheep from the goats. To the sheep at his right hand he says: "You have my Father's blessing; come, enter and possess the kingdom that has been ready for you since the world was made. For when I was hungry, you gave me food; when thirsty, you gave me drink; when I was a stranger you took me into your home, when naked you clothed me; when I was ill you came to my help, when in prison you visited me." (Matt. 25:34–36, NEB.) But some of the sheep suddenly find themselves on the right hand of the Lord and *do not know why*. In utter astonishment they ask him: "Lord, when was it that we saw you hungry and fed you, or thirsty and gave you drink, a stranger and took you home, or naked and clothed you?

When did we see you ill or in prison, and come to visit you?" (Vs. 37–39.) *Lord, when?* I am afraid there has been some mistake; it was not us; we do not deserve this. But the Son of Man answered: "I tell you this: anything you did for one of my brothers here, however humble, you did for me." (V. 40.) Christ is found in every man, in every human hand and face. He is met incognito—in places and persons where he is not expected—in the hungry, the thirsty, and the naked, the sick man and the prisoner. Christ is not met as a superhuman wonder-worker who gives us no choice but to accept him; he comes instead as one of our brothers, as one who needs our help, or as the gracious neighbor who stretches out his hand to give us help in the darkest hour. He comes into our lives as the stranger—just as Jesus came into the lives of his disciples on the road to Emmaus—*unrecognized*. He comes as the "man existing for others,"[7] recognized not by who he is but by what he does, as Jesus was finally recognized in the breaking of bread.

In traditional Christian terms, the "incarnating" universe is the body of Christ, a world transfigured by the Word which is "the true light that enlightens every man" (John 1:9). But the Christian church has not only failed to grasp the absolute *totality* of the incarnation; it has actually limited this "incarnating" by identifying *itself* as the body of Christ. It is obvious, then, that the church, in confronting the world in the guise of the body of Christ, has committed the primal heresy: it has annihilated the *universality* of the incarnation. Thus it is no surprise that the Christian church has largely failed to proclaim the incarnational God who is Love, and has instead endeavored to force the rest of the world into servile obedience to the monarchic Creator God—the infinitely distant, wholly Other, Lawgiver and Judge.

In the "incarnating" universe there is no room for the "in" group and the "out" group—no possibility of separating the rest of humanity from the love of God. In the Old Testament it was prophesied by the prophet Joel that the time would come when God would pour out his Spirit "on all flesh" (Joel 2:28). Thus, at the time of Pentecost, when Peter first stood up to proclaim the gospel, he began with these words from Joel, announcing categorically that the Spirit was now poured upon *all men*. God is now revealed in everyone—Jew and Gentile, Communist and Christian and Chinaman, Buddhist and Hindu and Moslem, infants, infidels, sinners, and saints. To claim less is to limit God's unending love. Everything that man is and does is God "being" and "doing"; as Blake wrote in *The Marriage of Heaven and Hell,* "God only Acts & Is, in existing beings or Men." Nature is God in the act of "naturing," man is God in the act of "manning," man surfing or sky-diving or orbiting in space or just walking along is God "incarnating." The very stars are the "starring" of God, and all of life is the "living" of God. Man experiencing God is God experiencing man, for, as Meister Eckhart said, "the eye with which I see God is the same eye with which God sees me."[8] The whole universe is the "acting" and "being" of God—that is, God "othering" himself, being what he is not, just as Hamlet is an actor being what he is not.

And all of this God talk is man "godding"—pretending to be what he is not. For when man separates himself from the rest, pretending to be a separate ego, a separate God appears, but when man unites himself to the rest, God (dis-)*appears in*(-to) the All that is One and *ex-ists* (comes out) in the Uni-verse that is All-One INCARNATING.

7

The Indwelling Spirit

Christianity began with the Easter event. Out of the darkness one Friday, out of the despair and defeat at Golgotha, there came a new and astonishing proclamation about Jesus of Nazareth, announcing the decisive act of God: "The Jesus we speak of has been raised by God, as we can all bear witness. Exalted thus at God's right hand, he received the Holy Spirit from the Father, as was promised, and all that you now see and hear flows from him." (Acts 2:32–33, NEB.) The loss of faith and dispersion of the disciples immediately before Easter indicate that the historical Jesus was not enough to change men completely. Yet the total transformation of these men, and those who heard them, is without precedent in history—and this transformation is the result of Easter. The thorny question is: What happened?

The historical events and concrete details of Easter are quite beyond the power of the historian to verify. Moreover, the Biblical record is so contradictory that historical reconstruction seems impossible. Every "harmony" of the Gospels results in imponderable questions, irreducible contradictions, or total failure. Yet these contradictions are the surest proof of the validity of the accounts, for absolute consistency might well be rejected by a modern court as a sure sign that a deliberate hoax was being perpetrated.

Variations in detail surround all the central questions of Easter. Who saw Jesus first? How many times did he appear? Where did he appear? What did he say and do? What was the nature of the appearance? According to Matthew, the risen Lord appeared some ninety miles from the tomb, in Galilee (Matt. 28:16–17), and the disciples were directed there according to Mark (Mark 16:7), though no appearances are recorded. Luke and John place all the appearances at the tomb or near Jerusalem. How is this disparity to be resolved? Every Gospelist records that Mary Magdalene was among the first who visited the tomb, but Matthew, Mark, and Luke disagree on who was with her at the time. John says she visited the tomb alone. And again: Mark records that the tomb was not entered, whereas John records that it was not only entered but found to contain the funeral wrappings of Jesus—intact. And, finally, the appearance of Jesus was at once physical enough to eat "a piece of broiled fish" (Luke 24:42) yet spiritual enough to be unrecognized on the road to Emmaus, and to "vanish" suddenly from sight (Luke 24:31).

When we turn to the book of The Acts we find Stephen, a moment before being stoned to death, having a vision of the risen Lord: "Gazing intently up to heaven, [he] saw the glory of God, and Jesus standing at God's right hand." (Acts 7:55–56, NEB.) Paul's experience of the risen Lord on the road to Damascus is still stranger: "Suddenly a light from heaven flashed upon him. And he fell to the ground and heard a voice . . . . The men who were traveling with him stood speechless, hearing the voice but seeing no one." (Acts 9: 3–4, 7.) And this experience of Paul's, it should be noted, took place at least *seven years after* the crucifixion! In describing it later, Paul said he had been

"caught up to the third heaven," where he had seen
"visions and revelations of the Lord" and "heard things
that cannot be told, which man may not utter" (II Cor.
12:1–4). In his letter to the Galatians he wrote: "It
pleased God . . . to reveal his son *in me* [*en emoi*], that I
might preach him among the heathen." (Gal. 1:15–16,
KJV; note the mistranslations: *"to* me," RSV, and *"to* me
and *through* me," NEB!)

The Easter event was *real*, but indescribable—things
that cannot be told, which man may not utter. Thus everyone described it in his own way. And because Easter was a
transforming subjective encounter, the problem arose of
how to clothe it in objective language, how to contain the
untellable in a tale of words. Thus, from the start, Easter
was clothed in the colorful language of myth and symbol.
The *real* Easter event lies behind these myths, and must
not be confused with them. Nevertheless, we must come to
the Easter event through these myths; there is no other
way.

The actual occurrence that I have called the Easter
event includes *what happened* and *what was experienced*
by the disciples. To this Easter event at least two sets of
interpretive myths have been attached. The first of these
is the myth of resurrection, which is generally taken as the
event itself, rather than an interpretation of it. The second
mythical cluster includes the myth of the ascension of
Jesus into heaven, and Pentecost, the descent of the Holy
Spirit into the midst of human life. Ascension and Pentecost have likewise been confused with actual historical
events, though not with Easter itself. Thus Christianity
maintains that three separate events occurred after Jesus'
death—resurrection, ascension, and Pentecost—whereas
these are mythical interpretations of a *single* Easter event.

In dealing with the resurrection as myth, we must face at

least two problems. On the one hand, there is the mistaken notion held by most Christians that "myth" means "untrue," "unhistorical," "imaginary," or "fanciful." Naturally they object, believing that the label "myth" is a dismissal of Easter as untrue. On the other hand, even among those who are knowledgeable about the mythical nature of much of the Bible (the seven-day creation, the virgin birth, etc.) there is a strong reluctance to include resurrection as part of that mythology. Theologians have always emphasized the *historical* nature of Christianity, and Westerners generally insist on having a religion with a kind of "scientific" validity to it, that is, a religion based on real events. The main point, then, is that calling the resurrection "myth" is not calling the Easter event "myth." It is simply to recognize the difference between history and the interpretation of history. Indeed, the myth of resurrection is precisely what lifts the temporal event of Easter into a timeless truth where it can mean something for all time. In short, the resurrection as myth is by no means "mere" myth; on the contrary, it is rescued from the fate of being "mere" history or "mere" fact.

What, after all, would be the meaning of the resurrection if it *were* a historical event? Again, we are faced with the problem of how one historical event among many can have a decisive effect for the whole of history. Moreover, to reduce the resurrection to a fact is to make it into a physical proof, a miraculous "sign," which Jesus refused to give. Man's free response to Christ becomes a forced response in the face of this kind of evidence. Moreover, belief is then based on the ability of God to reconstruct matter so that what was "dead" comes "alive." As such, faith is based on a kind of ghost story and the mystery of a missing corpse, a fantastic claim that not only breaks God's own laws but insults the workings of the divine.

Paul Tillich called this view "absurdity . . . compounded into blasphemy."[1] Werner and Lotte Pelz have put it this way: "To treat the Resurrection as an *historical event* is to misunderstand the meaning both of history and Resurrection. History is concerned with the past, the fixed, the dead. Resurrection is concerned exclusively with the future, the moving, the living."[2] What, then, is the meaning of resurrection—as myth?

Extensive anthropological research has shown that the myth of resurrection was common to nearly all the great Mediterranean cultures that predate Christianity. In the myths of Tammuz, Osiris, Adonis, Attis, and Persephone, the ancient Sumerians, Egyptians, Babylonians, and Greeks expressed their awareness of the seasonal decay and revival of life throughout nature: the mystery of death and rebirth. Christianity was thus born into a cultural setting where the myth of resurrection was a well-known symbol for one of the great unknowns of existence.

In the mythology of the ancient Sumerians, Tammuz appears as a familiar youthful lover of the mother goddess, Ishtar, who embodied the forces of reproduction. According to the myth, Tammuz died and passed away to the nether regions of the dead each year, where his lover, goddess Ishtar, quickly followed in quest of him. While she was away, all love activity ceased on earth: men and animals forgot to reproduce themselves, and nature waned to near extinction. In the underworld, however, Ishtar was sprinkled with the water of life by the queen of the infernal regions and was allowed to depart with Tammuz to the world above. Upon their arrival on earth, all nature revived. Tammuz was intimately linked to plants that fade away each year, and his death was apparently mourned annually with the sorrowful playing of the flute in the

month of Tammuz. Natural events were thought to follow
the divine pattern; the sprinkling of the water of life in the
underworld was celebrated by sprinkling water on the
ground, and the appearance of the green shoots in spring
was worshiped as the reappearance of Ishtar and Tammuz
from the realm of the dead beneath the earth.

Virtually all resurrection myths follow this pattern. In
Greek mythology, Persephone too is rescued from the
underworld, but having been fed pomegranate seeds by
Hades, she must return to the underworld for half of each
year. Since Persephone was linked to the grain harvest,
specifically corn, her seasonal appearance was responsible
for the seasonal appearance of a new crop. The worship of
Adonis originated with the Semitic peoples of Babylonia
and Syria and was borrowed by the Greeks around the
seventh century B.C. There is archaeological evidence that
rites were carried out at Byblus in Syria and Paphos in
Cyprus. The worship of a similar god, Attis, originating in
the ancient Turkish province of Phrygia, eventually found
its way to Rome in 204 B.C. A prophecy in the Sibylline
Books suggested that Rome would be freed from her
Carthaginian oppressors if the goddess Cybele, mother of
Attis, were brought to Rome. Ambassadors were quickly
dispatched and soon returned with Cybele's sacred black
stone to Rome, where it was installed in the Temple of
Victory on the Palatine hill. The prophecy worked: Han-
nibal was repulsed the following year, and Italian farmers,
presumably because of the influence of the vegetation god
Attis, recorded a record harvest that summer!

In ancient Egyptian mythology, Osiris was the nature
deity who annually died and was reborn. Osiris was not
only connected with the seasonal cycle; his resurrection was
supposed to be the pledge to all men of resurrection beyond

the grave. The famous mummification rites were an attempt to duplicate the funeral of Osiris so that each individual would follow Osiris to life everlasting.

It is perfectly clear that the resurrection was a mythic interpretation of the mystery of life and death through the entire Mediterranean world. In the face of the Easter event, then, it was almost inevitable that this myth from surrounding cultures would be applied to it. As Tillich says:

> In the moment in which Jesus was called the Christ and the combination of his messianic dignity with an ignominious death was asserted—whether in expectation or in retrospection—the application of the idea of resurrection to the Christ was almost unavoidable. . . . The character of this event remains in darkness, even in the poetic rationalization of the Easter story. . . . A real experience made it possible for the disciples to apply the known symbol of resurrection to Jesus, thus acknowledging him definitely as the Christ.[3]

In purely naturalistic terms, the myth of resurrection is not about a single event in the past. In all its variations, the rebirth of the rising god and nature is celebrated annually. Moreover, the idea of rebirth is one that is applied to all nature—to the entire universe. But once the dichotomy between the "divine" and the "natural" disappears, resurrection is seen to be what the whole universe does in the present moment. We may describe it as RESURRECTING. The whole cosmos is moving in a process describable as "resurrecting," and we may speak of the "resurrecting" universe.

Traditionally, Christianity has found the resurrection to hold the final answer to sin and death. It was through the sin of the first Adam that death entered human life; but it is through the Second Adam, Christ, that God's "act of grace . . . issued in a verdict of acquittal" (Rom. 5:16,

NEB). For Christ achieved God's holy purpose by making himself nothing, assuming the nature of a slave, humbling himself, and accepting death by crucifixion (Phil. 2:7–11). Out of this complete obedience and perfect sacrifice the very power of sin and death has been annulled, for Christ rose from the dead. By letting the power of evil do to him all it could—by letting death utterly destroy the incarnate Word—and then by rising to life again, the Lord has shown that "death is swallowed up; victory is won! O Death, where is your victory? O Death, where is your sting?" (I Cor. 15:54–55, NEB).

Now despite the assertion that Christ's resurrection annulled the power of sin and death, they have remained somewhat problematic in Christian thinking. Sin is, after all, not something that the perfectly good God should have allowed, and death seems to be a crushing blow in a world reportedly made for man's complete happiness. Out of this problem many questions arise: How is evil, whether it be sin or death or any other kind, possible in a universe made by an absolutely good God? Why does the omnipotent God not prevent evil? Does evil come from God (in which case he is surely satanic), or does it arise on its own (in which case God has lost control, or is not all-powerful)? Or does evil come from Satan? And if so, who made Satan? God? Or did Satan create himself—in which case we really have two "Creators," one good and one evil?

The existence of evil, however, is always set in contrast with the idea of God's Creation, a Creation that was "good" in the eyes of the Lord. But there is no way to resolve the existence of evil in a "good" universe created by a "good" God who is all-powerful, all-knowing, and utterly transcendent. This formulation of the problem, however, neglects the fact that this doctrine of Creation was only the *beginning* of Hebrew understanding. Each later mythical story of the Bible is a retelling of the story of Creation with progressively deeper understandings.

Creation, as noted earlier, began in terms of a Producer producing a product. The incarnation, however, refines this, so that "creating" takes place by "incarnating," by the Produced "becoming" the product. The "incarnating" universe is the Actor "acting" or the Dancer "dancing." Yet even the idea of "incarnating" is only a partial description; the final vision of the "creating" activity comes in the idea of the sacrificing of God. When God is seen as making the universe, he can be held responsible for every flaw in the workmanship, especially evil. But once God is understood as "incarnating" the universe, his participation in evil becomes obvious. For the "incarnating" universe is not controlled by a distant God: it is actually created by God surrendering himself and becoming the world. Creation is the sacrifice of the One for the All, the creation of the whole universe by "the Lamb [Christ, or the Word] slain from the foundation of the world" (Rev. 13:8, KJV). Sacrifice, then, is the archetypal symbol or analogy, not only for what man must do for God but also for what God has done for man. In its deepest understanding, this is what is meant by the "death of God": God must die if man is to live. An incarnational theology demands it.

Yet if we follow the meaning of "creating" by "incarnating" to its limit, it becomes apparent that the divine sacrificing is so *complete,* so totally sacrificial, that it finally involves the tragedy of existence, decay, and death. Anything short of God's *complete* "incarnating" of the flesh would be imperfect creation and mock incarnation. Thus "incarnating" must, of necessity, include more than bringing order out of chaos, more than the joyous birth of a child in a manger—it must ultimately include the destruction and death of that order, and of that child. And so the cross. The "incarnating" of the divine in the human ultimately destroys the divine, for the total process of Creation is Creation-incarnation-destruction—or, in a new processive language, CREATING-INCARNATING-DESTROYING. And the final fulfillment of the "creating-destroying" universe is the RESURRECTING universe, the cosmos RE-CREATING out of the ashes of its own destruction.

Christian theology has always centered on the God who stands for creation, production, and the establishment of the "good" and "perfect" upon the primordial rock and fire of the suns. By defining Evil—the power of destruction, the decay of the good and perfect—as God's opposite, the unity of "creating-destroying" as a single world process has been missed. Evil, decay, death, Satan, and hell have therefore been a positive danger to theology, never satisfactorily integrated into a total design. But, in fact, as Alan Watts points out, "life and death are not opposed but complementary, being the two essential factors of a greater life that is made up of living and dying just as melody is produced by the sounding and silencing of individual notes."[4] Here we could profit enormously by certain insights from Indian and Chinese philosophy. In Hinduism, Brahma the Creator, Shiva the Destroyer, and Vishnu the Preserver are different faces of the One, Brahman. The whole universe, whether creating or destroying, is thus seen as a continuous "incarnating" activity of the One who is Brahma-Vishnu-Shiva. In the words of Ananda K. Coomaraswamy, "the Solar hero and the Dragon, at war on the open stage, are blood brothers in the green room."[5]

In Taoism, the Way of Nature (*tao*) is symbolized in the perfect circle divided between Yang and Yin—the White and the Black, Good and Evil, Creation and Destruction. The Yang-Yin symbol stands as the supreme symbol for the simple fact that opposites are related to each other and cannot exist apart. The *tao,* the pattern of the universe, is therefore the alternation of Yang and Yin, the continual destruction of Yang by Yin, the continual creation of Yang out of Yin. The parallel in Christianity to Brahma-Shiva or Yang-Yin is, of course, *God-Satan!* And after all, is Satan not Luci-fer, the "light bearer," a fallen *angel* whose role is to do the dirty work of the Lord, the secret partner who makes a deal with God over the body of Job? "Thus," asks Alan Watts, "if Christ sits at the right hand of God, who sits at the left?"[6]

To understand the whole cosmos as "creating-destroy-ing-resurrecting" is to catch a vision of the most amazing spectacle there is—the panorama of life itself. "Resur-recting" is the visible process of day emerging out of night, spring rolling out of winter, living things growing out of the dead matter of their forerunners. The whole universe is one huge "destroying-creating" organism, rising like the im-perishable phoenix out of the ashes of its own conflagra-tion. Worlds evolve from star dust only by the destruction of a star. Life grows out of a chemically rich sea surface only by consuming those chemicals. The destruction of fins is the creation of legs; the destruction of legs is the creation of wings. Life evolves by destroying itself and recreating itself, just as a mother's body starves itself to feed an unborn child. And when Christians assert that the whole universe is founded on sacrifice and that God is Love, they mean precisely this: that every new creation arises out of the self-emptying (kenosis) of the divine Word—the "pattern of all the heavenly" (I Cor. 15:48, NEB)—into the PATTERNING of existing things. Divin-ity is not everlasting Permanence, rock-hard stability, but eternal love—a soft and yielding flow of star dust through intricate designs of fern and flesh, a melodious ripple of chemistry into pheasant and philosopher, a fluid pattern of energy stretching from atom to galaxy. And every flow, every ripple and pattern, is a "re-creating," a "resurrecting."

What does faith in the resurrection mean? Above all, it does not mean that man survives death. It does not mean that the selfish, nasty little egos men cling to and boast about and try to preserve are destined for everlasting life. Life emerges out of death, but it is not "this" life or "that" life, but life—or *living*. If the sacrifice of the divine in becoming flesh is *total*, how can man expect to sacrifice less? The life that emerges out of death is *new* life, unrecognized, even as Christ was unrecognized on the road to Emmaus. What is meant by faith in the resurrection is faith in the ever-moving flow of the "creating" process. Out of death new life *must* come. Level this world down to the animal kingdom and "man" will emerge again. Level this world down to nothing but the sea, and life will appear again. Level the whole cosmos down to hydrogen dust in space, and stars will shine again. Buried weeds will not remain buried; suppressed emotion agitates until it explodes; minority groups rise in arms almost in the midst of extinction; suppressed nations assert themselves—for life fights its way out of death again and again. Crucify "the image of the invisible God," the very "wisdom of God," and that Wisdom, the pattern of the heavenly, will rise again to "fill the universe" (Col. 1:15, I Cor. 1:24, RSV; Eph. 4:10, NEB). For the "resurrecting" universe is a universe of harmonious flow where every day is a new dawn and every creation is a dramatic re-creation beyond belief.

Resurrection means for man not the security of ultimate escape from the world, but the certainty that life has meaning because there is death, and the wisdom of know-

ing that life is only possible where there is death. Understood this way, the universe is not a rusty, clanking
machine but a moving, flowing, re-creating melody where
each note is released into the silence and each silence is the
birthplace of a new note. Man in the "resurrecting" universe is man "resurrecting" with it, riding the creative
crest of existence on a gigantic surfboard on which the
greatest ride is in the chaos beneath the curl, where the end
is always annihilation beneath a sea of foam, and where
man always reappears far out at sea, riding the crest again.

In terms of Easter, this vision of man is neither that of
a wispy, walking, resurrected spirit, nor a ghostly, emaci-
ated corpse resuscitated from the dead, but Man the
divine—the Exalted Lord! And this is precisely what
Easter is about, for the myth of resurrection was applied
to Easter rather late, perhaps thirty years after the event.
But long before Easter was clothed in resurrection symbolism, it was connected with other myths—the myth of
the ascension into heaven, and the myth of Pentecost. The
first understanding of the Easter event was that of the
Exalted Lord, Man made divine.

The first record of the Easter event is found in Paul
(I Cor. 15:3–8), in a concise, formulaic paragraph, which
may be the remnant of an early oral creed. Paul simply
says that "Christ died for our sins . . . , was buried, . . .
was raised . . . , and appeared to Cephas, then to the
twelve. Then he appeared to more than five hundred
brethren at one time . . . . Then he appeared to James,
then to all the apostles. Last of all, as to one untimely
born, he appeared also to me." Paul appears to be talking
about a resurrected ("raised") Christ, except that he includes his own experience on the road to Damascus, later
described in terms of a vision of the Exalted Lord (II
Cor. 12:1–4). This experience, according to informed

scholarship, occurred no earlier than A.D. 35, some seven years after the crucifixion.[7] Paul, then, apparently knew nothing of the later ascension tradition in which Christ was exalted into heaven, bringing *an end* to the appearances. For him, the Exalted Lord was an eternal reality, a reality that he himself had encountered long *after* the crucifixion and which he believed had been encountered long *before* it, during the exodus. "For they [the Israelites] drank from the supernatural Rock which followed them, and the Rock was Christ." (I Cor. 10:4.) For Paul, then, the Easter event was never a fixed historical event, a resurrect-*ion,* but always a continual possibility in the here and now, a vision in the timeless moment of eternity, a resurrect-*ing.*

Once it is clear that Paul's experience was of the exalted (Ascended) Lord, his puzzling statement that the risen Lord "appeared to more than five hundred brethren at one time" (I Cor. 15:6) becomes clear. Recorded nowhere in the Gospels, this mass appearance points toward the event behind Luke's story of Pentecost in Acts, ch. 2, where a large number of citizens were converted at the time when the disciples were "filled with the Holy Spirit" (v. 4). In the earliest Christian experience, then, the Easter event was understood not only in terms of resurrection but also in terms of ascension and Pentecost. Separated into three separate, historical "events" in later tradition, these mythical interpretations all referred originally to Easter, and were, in fact, equivalent to it.

A close examination of the *later Gospel accounts* makes clear that Easter-as-Ascension and Easter-as-Pentecost are interpretations deeply embedded in these accounts *alongside* the later traditions of open tomb and disappeared corpse. Thus Mark records that "the Lord Jesus, after he had spoken to them, was *taken up into heaven,* and sat down at the right hand of God. And they went forth and preached everywhere, *while the Lord* [i.e., the Spirit] *worked with them* and confirmed the message by the signs that attended it" (Mark 16:19–20, italics added). Here, in the earliest Gospel, is a perfect coalescence of resurrection, ascension, and the Spiritual Presence of Pentecost in a single experience. The Gospel of Matthew likewise ends with the words of the risen Lord: "Lo, I am with you always, to the close of the age" (Matt. 28:20), a promise that identifies the resurrection with the Presence of the Spirit. Luke too says that while the risen Lord "blessed them, he parted from them, and was carried up into heaven" (Luke 24:51); and his later narrative in The Acts specifically links Easter and the Spiritual Presence: "In the first book, O Theophilus, I have dealt with all that Jesus began to do and teach, until the day when he was taken up, *after he had given commandment through the Holy Spirit* to the apostles whom he had chosen." (Acts 1:1–2, italics added.) Likewise, the Gospel of John links these three events as one. On Easter morning, when the risen Lord was met by Mary, he said to her, "Go to my brethren and say to them, *I am ascending* to my Father" (John 20:17, italics added). Later that same day the risen Lord "breathed on them, and said to them, 'Receive the Holy Spirit'" (John 20:22). Every account of Easter agrees, then, that resurrection, ascension, and Pentecost were one event. Thus the ascension and Pentecost account in The Acts—usually thought of as two *additional* events—must be seen as an Easter account. And this interpretation is verified by Peter's first sermon, when he proclaimed that "the Jesus we speak of has *been raised* by God, as we can *all bear witness. Exalted thus* at God's right hand, he received the Holy Spirit from the Father, as was promised, and all that you now see and hear flows from him" (Acts 2: 32–33, NEB, italics added).

The symbols of ascension and the Exalted Lord have been the most misunderstood of New Testament symbols. Properly understood, the self-emptying of God into the flesh of man is the self-annihilation of the supernatural Lawgiver and Judge. The incarnation is therefore the dramatic death of the distant Lord, which means not so much that "Jesus is Lord" as that "the Lord is Jesus." Traditional theology has, however, missed the self-sacrificial death of the distant Lord, allowing him to be, quite literally, *resurrected* as the Exalted Lord. Thus the Exalted Christ in heaven has become another monarchic Lawgiver and Judge, condemning men to hell, breaking open the Judgment Book, and legislating the universe like the morally intolerable "Hound of Heaven" that he replaced. It is perfectly clear that the traditional emphasis on Christ as God, rather than God as Christ, actually reverses the real thrust of the incarnation. For the Exalted Lord is still the Lord apart, out there, rather than "God with us." Thus the symbol of the Exalted Lord must mean something quite different if it is to be rescued from the mere reassertion of the supernatural God.

Just as the "sin" of Adam means the sin of *all* mankind and the Word becoming flesh refers to *all* flesh, so too does the Exalted Man refer to *all* men. For Christ is the Second Adam: "If the wrongdoing of that one man brought death upon so many, its effect is vastly exceeded by the grace of God and the gift that came to so many by the grace of the one man, Jesus Christ" (Rom. 5:15, NEB). The incarnation of the Word in the flesh and the ascension of Christ into heaven ultimately obliterate the gulf between "heaven" and "earth." In the incarnation, the "flesh" of this world is made holy, nature is sanctified; and in the ascension, man himself is divinized and "christened." As Athanasius said, "He became man that we might be made God."[8]

Yet, when man becomes God, when man is "exalted," he does not become a supernatural "God in heaven," a King of kings, or Ruler of the universe. He becomes a living spirit, for exaltation and the outpouring of the Spirit are the same thing. The "ascension" of the risen Lord into "heaven"—which Jesus said was *within*—is the birth of that "Lord" who is the INDWELLING Spirit, in the heart of man himself. And here the meaning of Easter—Ascension and Pentecost—breaks out of the realm of the "historical" event and into the realm of that timelessness which is eternity, since the birth of the Spirit in man is the *real*-izing or dis-covering of the Spirit that has been within man from the beginning. For the Spirit of man is God's breath, the *ruach Adonai* that was breathed into the first Adam when "man became a living being" (Gen. 2:7). We finally understand that breath to be the Holy Spirit that dwells with us when Christ—"the last Adam . . . , a life-giving spirit" (I Cor. 15:45)—dwells in us. "For we are the temple of the living God." (II Cor. 6:16.)

Thus, the final vision of the "incarnating" universe begins to unfold itself in the moment when the absent God, the silent God, the Lawgiver and Judge in heaven, is annihilated in flesh and obliterated in crucifixion—only to ascend as the living Spirit of man himself. The distinctions between "God" and the "world," the "Word" and the "flesh," which we have so far submerged artificially by process language ("creating," "incarnating") are now seen to be the same distinctions that are obliterated *by God himself,* in his final "revealing" of himself as the "indwelling" Spirit of man.

From this point of view, the final revelation of the divine and the deepest mystery of evolutionary science

meet in the most unexpected place—the Spirit of man.
For the creation of man out of star dust is the growth of
Spirit out of nature. The whole de-veloping of the universe
is the un-folding of matter so that what has been closed is
now dis-closed, what is "deep" comes to the "surface." The
hidden qualities of hydrogen are revealed in a hundred
complex elements, which in turn evolve by turning inside
out, pro-ducing living chemistry, light-responsive protoplasm, and all the subsequent refinements of awareness,
self-awareness, and transcendent Spirit. A new meaning
for the "love" and "patience" of God is thus revealed, for
God sacrifices himself so totally as to remain in bondage,
"covered" in the chaos of unorganized matter from the
stars, waiting for the "dis-covery" of himself by man and in
man. And this unveiling of Spirit at the center of this
world—in the primal chaos of interstellar star dust, in the
seething waters of the Precambrian ocean—is precisely
what the Biblical doctrine of the "indwelling" Spirit is
about. For, in the beginning, while the earth was without
form, before the "creating" Word had called the light out
of darkness, the Spirit (*ruach,* wind, or breath) of God
"was moving over the face of the waters" (Gen. 1:1–2).
Transpose the image of *over* to *within* and it is found that
this is precisely what the primordial Spirit of the "creating," evolving universe is all about: the "Breath of Life"
that turns man into a living being, the inner Word IN-
SPIRING the prophets and poets, the OUTPOURING
Wind of the day of Pentecost, the INDWELLING Spirit
of the universal Body of Christ—all humanity.

Man is redeemed therefore by the crucifixion that gives
birth to Spirit, the crucifixion of the sinful "body of death"
(Rom. 7:24) that releases the Christ within. For those who
live in Christ "have crucified the flesh with its passions and
desires" (Gal. 5:24), "have been united with him in a

death like his" (Rom. 6:5), and have been raised from the dead to "walk in newness of life . . . , eternal life in Christ Jesus our Lord" (Rom. 6:4, 23). "The same God who said, 'Out of darkness let light shine,' has caused his light to shine within us" (II Cor. 4:6, NEB), so that we can cry with Paul, "I have been crucified with Christ; it is no longer I who live, but Christ who lives in me" (Gal. 2:20). And this redemption is not only from the body; it is from time, for man now discovers "an inner spring always welling up for eternal life" (John 4:14, NEB). Life in the Spirit is the giving up of life in the body and life in the mind, for when man lives in memory he lives in the past, and when he lives in anticipation he lives in the future, but when he simply *lives* he is in "the nick of time" where past and future meet, the timeless present. And eternal life is his.

If the final Reality called God is thus the "in-dwelling" Spirit, then the redeemed vision of the universe is the universe seen from the standpoint of Man "dwelling in" Spirit. From here, the still point, the whole cosmos is aflame with divinity, a majestic sacred glitter brighter than the jewelled throne of heaven. For this is precisely where the Spirit dwells—in the inner Kingdom of Heaven: "Surely you know that you are God's temple, where the Spirit of God dwells" (I Cor. 3:16, NEB). And I AM that Spirit. And every time a new being says "I AM," the "only-begotten Son" is "resurrecting" again, for Christ is that one and only "light that enlightens every man" (John 1:9)—"incarnating" in every moment of time. Suddenly the truth dawns that I am "creating" the world, I am "incarnating" my own flesh, I am "dwelling in" Spirit and "pouring out" Spirit on all things, for God is "revealing" himself as the Christ Within who said, "Before Abraham was, I am" (John 8:58).

8

The Center Beyond Belief

As Wordsworth put it, "We murder to dissect."[1] Dissection gives man the answers about life he wants, except that they are "dead" answers. It is in the nature of living things to be curious. Children and kittens confirm it. But man is often fooled by his own answers. He fills the unthinkable Void with a thought, a supernatural God, deluding himself into thinking that every effect must have a cause, every action an agent, every time a beginning, every object a subject. He then fills these linguistic holes—agent, beginning, subject—with "God." He has not learned, as Wittgenstein said, that "there are, indeed, things that cannot be put into words. . . . What we cannot speak about we must pass over in silence."[2]

The most tragic form of this is found in Christian *e-ducation,* which should properly "lead out" the inner Spirit. From this point of view the lessons of the catechism are a disaster.

"Where did the world come from?"

"God made it."

"Oh."

Question asked, answer given, matter closed. The vague intimation of the unknown in the mind of the child is plugged up with a glib phrase; such an intimation, reaching beyond itself, may never appear again. Yet this is the sacrifice made every time a "religious" answer is given to a "scientific" or "philosophical" question, and it leads to a loss of the sense of wonder. We forget that there is a mystery to existence. We stifle the openness of a child's mind to the questions that, as adults, we no longer ask— supposedly to get the child's mind out of the clouds and onto the task at hand, that is, to make him functional. We miss the fact that a man who is functional but has lost his sense of wonder has lost what it is that makes him a man. This is not to advocate that we abandon "religion" in favor of "science." For science gets no closer to the mystery of the "creating" universe than the "religious" assertion that there is a "Creator." Indeed, science is overloaded with the insidious plausibility of its own kind of mythology—the mythology of scientism.

Primitive man, as noted earlier, saw everything in the universe as alive, and the celestial bodies of the heavens were so brilliant as to be virtually divine. Preliterate man in the forest simply knew of no way to account for the movements of the stars, the brilliance of the sun, or the waxing and waning of the moon other than attributing life to them. With the advent of civilization and the development of language, the animating spirits were gradually distinguished and separated from the mere stuff of the stars. The sun became a blazing chariot driven by Helios, the moon became the dazzling robes of Selene. Heavenly bodies became mere material "things" directed by independent heavenly spirits, gods, or goddesses. Then came science, reducing the star deities to "forces" and "laws" of nature, such as gravitational attraction and inertial motion. Yet gradually these "laws" were further reduced to statistical averages, and the so-called "forces" disappeared when it was seen that the stars are not "driven" at all, but simply take the line of least resistance. Yet, as if explaining the divine life of the stars was not enough, the gross stuff of which they were made was likewise analyzed away. The brilliance and sparkle, once thought to be the sign of divinity, turned out to be purely subjective—nervous patterns on the brain of man—and the movements of the stars turned out to be the changing position of the planetary observer. And finally, the "matter" of the stars was boiled away to virtually empty space, dotted with atomic particles, which were not really particles but waves, which in turn were not waves of something but simply wavings—imperceptible movements of we know not what, a singularization of a wave of probability. The celestial fireworks robed in divinity thus became something like a high-density emptiness!

As D. E. Harding put it, "Here is the murder story of all time—nothing less than 'cosmicide.' "[3] Just as theologians, mistaking religious myths for facts, have committed "deicide," the materialistic scientists, enthralled with their own mythology, have committed "cosmicide," reducing nature to a wasteland of bouncing bits and man to a cloud of atoms. In both cases man himself is reduced to the absurd. On the one hand, he becomes a helpless, cringing, sinful, disobedient ragamuffin so hopelessly lost that only the condescending grace of God can rescue him. On the other hand, he is reduced to a blind maelstrom of colliding waves, hopelessly spinning smoke rings and pipe dreams out of his own cosmic emptiness. In either case, it is "a tale told by an idiot, full of sound and fury, signifying nothing."

The fact is that a new point of view is in order, one that is neither "scientific" nor "religious" but simply the way we see things, that is, one in which *we* are central. For the stars could not have become ideas in the mind if the mind were not peculiarly powerful, nor could man have removed the star gods unless he were capable of hauling them away, presumably to another star. And he has done precisely that, for the divine beings "above" have disappeared and come alive on earth—in man's Spirit. If the heavenly brilliance and splendor of the sun and the moon are patterns in the mind, this is only proof that man holds the keys of the divine, for it is he who clothes things with divinity. Without life, and the emergence of man, there would have been no celestial beings, for the stars would never have been robed in divinity, the universe would never have become conscious of itself, and Spirit would never nod to Spirit from behind the eyes of every man.

At the heart of the dilemmas of science and religion is the accepted model of the universe, a model founded on a hierarchy of "levels" where man is a "body" controlled by a "mind," "earth" is a world controlled by "heaven," and "matter" is a stuff moved by "energy." But now we know that "mind" is inseparable from "body," since the mind is drastically altered by drugs and the body does intelligent things like growing eyeballs and fingerprints. Moreover, "matter" and "energy" are interchangeable, for "matter" is patterning energy and "energy" is radiating matter. But, having ex-plained, that is, "leveled out" the universe into a pile of bits, with "religious" ex-planations for some and "scientific" for the rest, we are now faced with developing a view of the Whole. Like a schoolboy faced with a dismantled clock, man not only has to get the pieces in the right order but get it to tell the correct time.

But the fact is that this is not a universe that does not work, like a broken clock. On the contrary, it works eminently well. The problem is not the universe itself, but our *model* of it. What we are fighting against is what

Wittgenstein called "the bewitchment of our intelligence by means of grammar."[4] The net we must escape is a conceptual one. But in fact we constantly *do* escape from it, whenever we look at the sea and listen to the wind without forcing them into a verbal net of explanation. As long as we are content to observe and describe the world without forcing it to be "scientific" or "religious" or anything else, but simply allowing it to *be,* we slip through the nets of culture and the grids of words. Like poets and painters, we create the world afresh when we allow ourselves to break free of habitual patterns and conventional bonds.

Life itself is the place to begin, if only because we ourselves are alive. To analyze the stars is fascinating, but the primordial stellar fires are a long way from the living essence of a man; thus we need to begin with him, for here we may find the clue that will unlock the secrets of the rest, including even the stars.

Life is the last frontier of the indefinable, the place where logic stops and wonder begins. Suppose the heart of a frog is cut out and placed in a jar of alcohol, a procedure that is followed in high school classrooms every day. What is there to "observe and describe"? There is perhaps all the magic this universe has to offer, for the heart will go on beating for many hours. And if the frog itself is prodded, it is found capable of twitching, kicking, and responding, even though the brain is destroyed and the heart removed.

Miracles have nothing to do with supernatural events, divine "incursions," freakish incidents. The real miracle is life itself. All but the most callous must be stirred to wonder by this experience. But what is the miracle of a living heart if "life" comes from some-thing else or somewhere else? For if "life" is some sort of "spark" that lives "in" things, that is "injected" into things at birth or conception, that "inhabits" them until death and then "leaves," then living things are nothing more than moving clay, intractible matter operated from some alien center—merely animated corpses. What man marvels at, then, is the traces of a power beyond this world, "giving" life to what is really just "inert" matter. If such were the case, the miracle would vanish, along with our wonder, for even the wonder in ourselves would turn out to be the animation of human dust by puppet strings from "above."

Somehow, man knows better. In everyday life he tends to be wiser than his "explanations" would indicate. He does not explain the miracle. Intuitively, he is drawn back to the twitching frog and the beating heart, rather than to a miracle from somewhere else. He is not drawn by something that is "given" life or "has" life: he is drawn by what is *living*. Moreover, he is not drawn *by* some power beyond, as if his body were an animated corpse of material "stuff"; he is drawn as a being who is essentially alive. And so he does not look "beyond" for the mystery. No matter what we have been told about "God," the "spark" of life, the breath of the divine, and no matter how much our words reflect outmoded divisions between material stuff and mental stuff, we know instinctively that there is nowhere else to look except at what is living, and that both "stuffs" are one stuff. For this is the mystery of plant cuttings that grow new roots, flower buds that open in a vase, cut fingers that grow new skin, and children's minds that bloom, apparently out of themselves. It is our innate wisdom that tells us that life is *within* that which lives without being different from it: that life is "living." It is this realization that leads us to examine things, to turn them over, feel them, and break them open to find out what is inside. For it is in the marvel of the perfectly folded leaf in the bud and the invisible blueprint for the pine tree within the cone that the true mystery of things resides.

Thus we come to the startling facts of growth and development. Out of an acorn comes an oak, out of the mushy grain of egg tissue comes a tadpole and then a frog, and out of the tiny seed in the human ovary comes a being that will someday ask, "Why?" Oaks and frogs and human beings have certain constant features by which they can be recognized, such as the characteristic pattern of an oak against the sky, the unusual jumping legs of the frog, and the erect walking position of a man. Yet each of these familiar patterns has grown out of a tiny group of cells that bears no resemblance to the final oak, frog, or man. The question therefore arises: How is it that a precisely formed, recognizable, apparently planned body rather than a formless mass is grown? This is a question that biologists have been working on for some decades, and one that has called forth answers of profound importance to our understanding of the entire universe.

In his book *The Biology of the Spirit*,[5] Edmund Sinnott describes simple biological experiments that anyone may perform, illustrating some of the most interesting features of life. When, for example, the branches of a white pine are bent and tied at a new angle to the trunk, adaptation sets in which tends to restore the characteristic *form* or shape of the tree. This adaptation is accomplished by the development of "reaction wood" along the bent branches. Reaction wood is characterized by shorter cells and denser structure, and consequently by the power to expand lengthwise as it grows. When a pine branch is bent, reaction wood develops along the inner side of the bend and, by gradual expansion, restores the branch to its original position. It would seem that some sort of plan for the entire tree is indelibly stamped on its cells, so that its growth is constantly regulated to a goal—a complete, mature tree. Moreover, there is no way in which we can give this "plan" a specific location within the tree; individual cells along the part of the tree that is injured seem to "know" what is to be done.

To say that the cells "know" how to grow a tree is not to attribute intelligence, in the human sense, to them. The fact is there is simply no way of describing this amazing quality of living things except by analogy with man's own behavior. It is perhaps worth noting that science, as well as religion, must use analogy to construct some kinds of explanation. Thus geranium plants not only seem to "know" how to make geranium plants, but every cell in the plant "knows." Consequently, a cutting consisting of only leaf cells or stem cells is able to produce roots and blossoms, suggesting that the plan for blossoms and roots is somehow stamped on every other cell of the plant. An organism is not only capable of regulating its own growth to a "goal"—a recognizably complete organism—but in some cases a "blueprint" for the entire organism is carried in every one of its parts. Sinnott concludes that "life is thus inherently goal-directed and purposeful."[6] As further evidence, he cites the experiment in which a certain type of sponge, belonging to the genus *Microciona,* having been squeezed through a fine mesh cloth and utterly disintegrated, was able in a few days to rebuild itself from the scattered fragments. An even more dramatic example is the construction within the cocoon of a butterfly from the decomposed remains of the silkworm. Each cell of the silkworm takes on a new function in the butterfly, a function totally unrelated to its function within the worm. Thus the intricately folded wings appear in the midst of the decayed flesh of the worm, a miracle of metamorphosis. Somehow the "plan" or ultimate "goal" of a butterfly is carried along in the cells of the worm.

Refusing to divide life into separate entities, into "body"

and "mind," Sinnott develops his thesis further: "Mental activity is far more varied and complex than bodily development, but both are rooted in the self-regulating and goal-seeking nature of protoplasm. All ideas at first were purposes. This concept interprets body and mind not as two unlike things but as two aspects of a fundamental unity."[7] This whole way of looking at psychology is highly suggestive. Understanding the growth and behavior of living things is no mere matter of moving chemicals about. The biologist's domain is exceedingly complex, for he is reaching into the very nature of the universe. As Herbert Spencer Jennings put it thirty-six years ago: "The great fact, the striking and characteristic feature of the biologist's picture of the world, is that biological materials include sensations, emotions, desires, hopes and fears, purposes, ideas, interest, thought, imagination, knowledge. Whatever else the universe may be, it is something that brings forth these things."[8] As well as bones and brains, life brings forth the fruits of the spirit: poetry and symphony, artistic imagination and mystical insight. Sinnott's final conclusion is inevitable: "Out of the harmonious rhythms of protoplasm come the physical processes of living things, the subject matter of biology; but from these same deep harmonies emerge as well the qualities of what we call the human spirit. Goal-seeking, creativeness, the power to mold matter to a purposed end . . . , refined and elevated far above its simple origin, and revealing heights and depths unguessed in lower forms, that is the manifestation of spirit."[9] The secrets of the human spirit are, then, somehow tied up with biological life.

Yet, what is life? It is tempting to define it as matter capable of directing its own behavior. Apart from the incredible problems of explaining this "directing," there is the disconcerting fact that nonliving matter apparently has the same ability. In 1955, scientists working at the Virus Laboratory of the University of California discovered that directive behavior extends to inert chemicals. By a complex process involving freezing, centrifuging, and chemical precipitation, these scientists successfully reduced the tobacco virus to a heap of inert chemicals incapable of infecting the tobacco leaf. When, however, these chemicals were brought together in a slightly acid solution and left for twenty-four hours, it was found that they had *rearranged themselves* into a living virus. "Directive" behavior therefore extends below the level of life, to chemistry itself.

Scientists have dealt with inanimate matter for so long that they have become accustomed to manipulating things from the outside. All the traditional experiments of the laboratory—and most of what goes on even in advanced physics—is of this nature: pouring solutions together, swinging pendulums, heating metals, bombarding metallic plates with beams of light or atomic particles. Matter has been seen in "chunks" and quantities that "have" certain physical and chemical qualities—nouns describable with adjectives. Preoccupied with gigantic, all-pervasive forces like gravitation and electromagnetism, engaged with the vast immensities of wheeling galaxies, red giants, and quasars, scientists have inadvertently ignored life. Not that biologists have not been working on life; certainly they have. But the *big* theories about reality, the cosmic theories, have been constructed as if separate from the man who constructs them. Consciousness, apparently only appearing in man, has been regarded as insignificant, an exception to the general rule, an aberration from the main trend of things, an epiphenomenon, or the expression of sheer mechanical principles—and thus left to the phenomenologists, behaviorists, and psychotherapists. The idea of explaining the whole universe by reference to man has simply been overlooked. Man, in the theory of relativity, for example, has been reduced to something like a fixed or moving point of view!

Yet this surface approach is gradually working itself to death. The idea that there are "things" that occupy space and have an "outside" is becoming suspect. The idea that there are "events" that go on between "things" is likewise becoming suspect. The idea that there are "qualities" attached to these "things" and "events" is becoming an untenable position. With the development of systems theory, biological ecology, and field analysis, the fallacy of separation is becoming apparent. The edges of things have become totally blurred, and the "outsides" of things have merged with the "insides" of their environment. Nothing is explained apart from the whole, and no whole is explained as a sum of its parts. Man, who once believed himself separate from the universe, has suddenly found himself involved in it. Every time he discovers a new principle in nature he finds a new pattern in his brain and has to learn a new pattern of living. Every shattered theory is a shattered mental concept and a broken self-image. Every meddling move man makes against the world around him turns out to rebound in his face. Instead of beating the universe into submission from above—from the *outside*—man now finds himself *inside* the universe. He himself is totally caught in the seamless robe, trying to pull a thread here and there without hanging himself. The universe as the *container* of man has become the challenge in our time, so that the heart of the universe is not somewhere else but is instead the heart also of man.

Thus while the stars are a million inaccessible miles deep to the core, there remain immeasurable depths in man's own spirit. The answers to the rest are there. In man is found an exceptional development of nerve, brain, mind, and spirit. What does this simple observation reveal about the rest? On the one hand, it may mean that man is an aberration from the general trend of things, a curiosity on the evolutionary tree not worth serious attention. On the other hand, his very uniqueness may be the key. Indeed, there is a distinct possibility that man is more than just an accidental scum on the cosmic stage; there is a teasing possibility that something *universal* is hidden beneath the exception. Have we perhaps neglected the possibility that the whole universe—and not just man—has an "inside" as well as an "outside"? In a remarkable passage, Teilhard de Chardin wrote:

> It is impossible to deny that, deep within ourselves, an "interior" appears at the heart of beings, as it were seen through a rent. This is enough to ensure that, in one degree or another, this "interior" should obtrude itself as existing everywhere in nature from all time. Since the stuff of the universe has an inner aspect at one point of itself, there is necessarily a *double aspect to its structure,* that is to say in every region of space and time—in the same way, for instance, as it is granular: *co-extensive with their Without, there is a Within to things.*[10]

What has so far been regarded as "dead matter" turns out to be far more "alive" than ever suspected. Beneath the external matter—beneath the visible appearance of swarming particles—we must assume a "biological" depth that is totally hidden and infinitely attenuated, but which is absolutely necessary to account for the "within" of man. As Teilhard de Chardin summarizes: *"In a coherent perspective of the world: life inevitably assumes a 'pre-life' for as far back before it as the eye can see."*[11] Scientists schooled in Newtonian physics, subscribing to mechanistic materialism, may well balk at such a conclusion, but there seems to be no choice. For, if all that man is has emerged accidentally from "inert" matter and "blind" energy, then life and consciousness are nothing but special forms of nonlife and unconsciousness—a conclusion that demands a very *un*scientific leap into the darkness of illogic and absurdity.

Biologists have long suspected as much. Fifty-five years ago, long before the major breakthroughs in virus research, J. S. Haldane pointed to life as the key to the universe: "As the conception of organism is a higher and more concrete conception than that of matter and energy, science must ultimately aim at gradually interpreting the physical world of matter in terms of the biological conception of organism."[12] In 1925, A. N. Whitehead wrote: "Science is taking on a new aspect which is neither purely physical, nor purely biological. It is becoming the study of organisms. Biology is the study of the larger organisms; whereas physics is the study of the smaller organisms."[13] Instead of reading forward from the whirling chaos of star dust, concluding that everything is gross, material, and unintelligent, biology has taught scientists to read backward from man, so that the whole universe is seen to be alive and intelligent. Thus, as J. W. N. Sullivan once put it, "amongst the new properties with which we propose to dower the atom, we shall probably have to include a rudimentary form of consciousness."[14]

The quest of the life and spirit of man therefore leads not only within him, to the chemicals of his biological being, but back in time to his roots in preconscious life. It leads down the ancient genetic path to sunlight and seashore, through the history of the primeval earth and the solar system to the ancient star dust out of which all things have come. It leads back to the stellar smelting furnaces,

down the atomic scale of the elements, along the very trail
of creation itself to the time when everything was hidden
in the dust of hydrogen. There, at the heart of the atom,
we reach the intangible, invisible, unspeakable, primordial
Reality, waiting to unfold.

An ancient Greek philosopher, Democritus (ca. 460–
360 B.C.), proposed the first "atomic" theory. Following
the Greek method of reliance on reason, he deduced that if
something were divided again and again, an end point
would eventually be reached when only indivisible particles called "atoms" would remain. "In reality," he said,
"there is nothing but atoms and space."[15] The Democritan
idea of "atoms and space" is essentially the modern idea of
"matter and space"—"things" made up of a permanent
and indestructible stuff occupying "space." This emphasis
on solid *things* and absolute *permanence* seemed eminently
"reasonable" to Democritus because it coincided with the
grammatical "logic of solids" inherent in his noun-oriented
language.

The scientific view of atoms some twenty-three centuries later, around 1900, was essentially no different.
Atoms were considered to be tiny "particles" attached together by tiny forces of "energy" somewhat akin to the
force of gravity. But again, the resulting popular image
of the atom as a miniature solar system, a duality of "particles" bound by "energy," is but another mental construction built on the grammatical division of "things" and
"events"—nouns and verbs. Recently, all of this has gone
by the board. "Ordinary matter" has vanished. The electron was first thought to be a highly charged particle, and
atomic scientists began to speculate as to how much of the
mass of the electron was due to its charge. When a measurement was finally made, the astounding result was that
the *whole* mass was electric charge. That was the begin-

ning. Soon it was found that matter could be turned into radiation, and that high-speed impacts of atomic particles could completely annihilate the particles in a burst of pure energy. The interchangeability of matter and energy according to Einstein's equation, $E = mc^2$, stated that the "energy" of a "thing" was equal to its mass multiplied by the speed of light squared! Without introducing the units of this formula, it is enough to see that the tiniest piece of stuff is equivalent to a phenomenal amount of energy. A thimbleful of mud, reduced to pure energy, could drive a train for thousands of miles; a few pounds could power every factory in the United States for weeks. And this energy, the most powerful force known, is the stuff of all things—including human flesh!

What then is an atom? Swing a golf ball around a football in a circle large enough to fill St. Peter's Cathedral, imagining all the Cathedral to be an atom, and we have a model of an atom. For an atom is mostly empty space, a fantastic illusion generated by electrons moving *so fast* that they are virtually everywhere at once. How fast? Physicists calculate that the electron revolves around its tiny nucleus at the speed of 6,570 thousand million revolutions per second. Pure energy, vibrating so fast as to actually produce the stuff we call matter: this is the grand Houdini act of all time, a cosmic deception so great as to make our heads spin. The whole world is thus a phantasmagoria, a flourish of pure power blazing forth in a pattern of "solid" matter, an unbelievable dizzy whirl of fluid energy evolving "things" virtually out of "no-thing."

The whole business is rather odd, downright mysterious, to say the least. For while the universe was dead stuff in solid chunks, it was under man's control; but now it has turned into a quantity of movement, a design of energy, creating activity—which means intelligent order. The prelife of the universe, the "within" of things, is shown in the very dance and patterning of electricity at the heart of all things—a brilliant display of sheer mindlike activity that literally brings forth everything from itself. The whole cosmos has turned into a dazzling sparkle of star dust—a suspension of pure light made into something solid by sheer "mentoid" power.[16] The universe turns out to be so structured, so intricately ordered, as to be beyond the farthest reaches of conscious thought: it is utterly "spiritual." Thus we arrive at what Robert Linssen has called "spiritual materialism"—a materialistic universe that is sustained by a vast, impalpable, never-erring spiritual energy—but with "matter" and "spirit" dissolved in a final unity that is beyond thought, imagination, or words.

In such a world, all the names given to the stuff of existence—whether we call it "atomic particles," "chemical molecules," "living protein," "vegetable cells," "animal matter," "nerve tissue," "electrical impulse," or "spiritual energy"—all come to a focal point in a magic land of transparent light where All is One and One is All, a center beyond belief. And, if we hold up a colored stone from the seashore, what can we make of it? Cold, solid, hard matter —but essentially it is a dancing pattern of light no different from the dancing energy of which the fingers that hold it are made. At the deepest level, both the pebble and the fingers are part of the same boundless ocean of energy, a place where energy "matters," a spot where the void is overruled. Moreover, everything that appears in man—life and mind and spirit—is implicit in the same colored stone. There is a whole universe of possibility hidden in every stone on the shore, as there is in all the common things of life, in the shells and earth and flowers.

> Flower in the crannied wall,
> I pluck you out of the crannies,

> I hold you here, root and all, in my hand,
> Little flower—but *if* I could understand
> What you are, root and all, and all in all,
> I should know what God and man is.
> > —*Alfred Lord Tennyson,*
> > *"Flower in the Crannied Wall."*

Primitive man in the magical forest tried to express the sheer wonder of this conception by his use of pure exclamation: *Mana! Orenda! Wakanda! Manitu! Mulunga!* The ancient Greeks tried to capture the many-faceted mystery of the universe by describing nature in terms of the movements of divine beings. The medieval Christians tried to capture the same reality in the grand symbolic structure of seven "realms" or "kingdoms"—the Great Chain of Being. All of these except the first were crudely spatial, analogies growing out of a spatially divided, classified universe. But as long as the universe was "leveled" into "realms" the primary problem was always that of expressing the interaction between the levels—how they were, in fact, related. In a hierarchical model of the universe, a model that is basically founded on the scheme of power politics, interaction always turns out to be a type of political interaction. Either the upper levels of the hierarchy "control" the lower levels, as the monarchic Lawgiver God controls the world, or the lower levels "revolt" against the upper levels, as Adam revolted against heaven in the primal act of pride. Movement in a political universe always turns into the machinery of the state. The tendencies of "control" and "revolt" run through the whole of modern philosophy: vitalism and mechanism, spiritualism and materialism, metaphysics and positivism, theism and naturalism. A political universe inevitably boils down to despotism or anarchy.

Yet, how are we to describe a world as richly varied

as this, where every star and flower and man is a meeting place for all that is? How can we conceptualize a universe where all that the universe has to offer is found in every one of its parts? How can we contain the whole within a single boundless contour? Perhaps the only possible language is that of poetry. But poetry is based on metaphor, and if one metaphor is now defunct, can another be found? Is there an image for the universe that can serve the needs of this century? Consider for instance a single nerve cell in the human body. In that one cell, at a tiny, almost invisible point, is discovered a marvelous organization. Atomic particles are found, combined into molecular structures, along with chemical activity within living protoplasm, and electrical energy passing from the brain with the seeds of a conscious message stamped upon its impulse—all these entwined together. How are we to describe a universe where everything is that complex?

I believe the needed metaphor is to be found in the work of Paul Tillich, in his conception of the "multi-dimensional unity of life."[17] Tillich's idea of reality as a multidimensional unity captures the interrelation of the separate aspects of the world in such a way that they are harmoniously related. Mutual interference is overcome; there is no control or revolt, since there are no separate levels or realms. Just as the dimensions of length, width, and height do not compete or interfere, but *meet* at the point of intersection, so too do the "dimensions" of matter and energy, chemistry and electricity, life and spirit, *meet* in total unity. Whereas the metaphor of levels emphasizes the *differences* between these realms, the metaphor of dimensions emphasizes the *unity* above the differences, relationship rather than separation, transaction rather than confrontation.

All the multitudinous facets of reality—whether they be seven or a thousand—may thus be considered as lines, or dimensions, that stretch away into the distance, in different directions at different angles, yet harmonize at the point of intersection, just as opposing threads enrich and support each other in the total design of a woven fabric. Such a metaphor expresses a changed vision of reality, a vision of diversity within unity. And, if every point in the entire universe is considered as just such a point of intersection—a place where all dimensions are potentially present, where some are actually present—the complex "things" of the world turn out to be a MANI-FESTING, a harmony of these dimensions in ever-new HAPPENINGS. Just as every point in space contains numerous radio frequencies, TV waves, sound and light waves, and cosmic rays from every corner of the universe, so too does every point in the universe contain potentially anything. From this standpoint, the entire universe is seen to be a seamless robe, an infinite harmony, a multidimensional unity where anything can happen, anywhere, anytime. Such a vision of reality is open-ended, for every dimension is a line stretching to infinity in both directions—indicating that new "developings" may yet enter into the total unity.

The colored pebble on the shore is, therefore, an interwoven pattern of all the dimensions of the cosmos, a fusing so rich in possibilities as to be beyond all analyses. Some dimensions are visible and tangible, some invisible and intangible because implicit and unmanifest. The absence of "life" is only the absence of actual life; potentially it is there, along with spirit itself. The whole cosmos is therefore an interlocking, transactional, harmonious sea of energy that appears here and there in the fiery globes of

the stars, the dewy globes of planets, and men, with all
their hopes and dreams and fears. And each a center
beyond belief.

What can be said about such a center? What can be said
about the beating heart of a frog or the emerging spirit
of man? One thing is certain: to separate out the various
dimensions, like the strands of a rope, and then to try to
relate them—as subject and object, agent and action,
cause and effect, things and events—through the awkward
use of the nouns and verbs of our "logical" grammar is to
destroy the harmony and reify the pattern into a host of
bouncing "things." Relating the different dimensions by
myths and symbols, through the grammatical devices of
analogy and metaphor, will work only so long as the myths
and symbols have cash value and do not become a barrier
to belief—that is, as long as they are taken "in the spirit,"
not literally.

There is, however, an alternative. When confronted with
a beating heart or a human spirit—when facing "something unknown . . . , doing we don't know what"[18]—it is
possible to simply "observe and describe" it in terms of
pure movement, process, and unexplained activity. Indeed,
this may be the only valid way of talking "theologically"
—or scientifically—without falling into explanations that
explain away or reductions that reduce reality to the absurd. Thus the universe is made up of ex-isting things,
things "coming out" of we know not what, manifesting
from an indescribable Center. For "things" are neither
static nor isolated: they are better described as EVENT-
INGS, FUSINGS, or COMBININGS. This understanding
of the world as dynamic change and process allows for
continual new "happenings," the endless surprises of a
"creating" and "re-creating" universe. And every new

"eventing" is the "in-carnating"—that is, the "em-body-ing"—of the Mystery all over again: a perpetual DESIGN-ING and PATTERNING of the Spirit into the visible things of the world. Thus, the solid *sub-stance* of the world turns out to be the fluid *under-standing* of the Spirit itself, for the world is seen as radiating from the Spirit, which is "standing under" and "dwelling in" all things, "dis-closing" and "dis-covering" itself as the Center of all "be-ing."

For this is the essence of the Christian vision: in Christ —who is the Logos, the Word and the Wisdom, the Light of the World, the Lord of the heaven within, the Spirit of man, and the Breath of life—"all things are held together" (Col. 1:17, NEB). We know God; we are at one with God "in the Spirit," that is, where our Center touches the Center of the "incarnating" universe. Here, there is but one "indwelling" Spirit. In the words of Emerson: "Within man is the soul of the whole; the wise silence; the universal beauty, to which every part and particle is equally related; the eternal ONE. . . . The heart in thee is the heart of all. . . . I am God in nature; I am a weed by the wall. . . . I—this thought which is called I—is the mould into which the world is poured like melted wax."[19]

9
Brahman and Tao

The deepest mystery of the universe is within it: the hidden Center that appears in the endless "creating" galaxies, the incredible "incarnating" activity of life and mind, and the ceaseless "resurrecting" of new life out of the old. No longer can we look for the foundation of this world somewhere else—up there, out there, or beyond. Advanced physics leads us from a divided world of "matter" and "energy" to a unitary concept of matter-and-energy as a single "designing." Biology leads us to "mind" as *minding*, "body" as *bodying*, and both united in a single *living*. And evolutionary studies find life and spirit implicit in the very dust and fire of the suns. We are thus led to the edge of thought and speech, where logic ends and poetry begins. Here we must resort to a model, a metaphorical picture, of the endless cosmic knot. Ancient images appear to serve us no more. A universe constructed on the political metaphor no longer fires our imagination, for the age of the kings is past. Whether the metaphor of "dimensions" will work depends on its imaginative power —its ability to "image" the unimaginable. In any case, it is simply a metaphor like any other—a device of the mind —and it too may soon be obsolete. Meanwhile, we must grasp its possibilities if we can.

Yet, having sorted through the whole "creating" universe of stars and life and mind, and having caught the unknown in the image of a "dimension," the mind is powerless, it seems, to go farther. The hidden dimension manifests itself only in terms of other dimensions, as "things" and "events." To put it into nouns and verbs is to describe the traces of something hidden—like Plato's shadows on the wall. The hidden dimension is "wholly other" in the cognitive sense: it is beyond understanding. Yet it is a "beyond in the midst of life,"[1] since it cuts through the visible world, invisibly, at every point. This hidden dimension is the "no-thing" behind all "things," the "no-event" behind all "events," the "word-less" reality behind all "words." It cannot be named or defined and, as such, someone may suggest, it is purely imaginary—a hypothesis that is inviolable because it can never be known.

Every attempt to communicate knowledge of this hidden dimension is doomed to failure from the beginning. Since words lead to reification and death by qualification, it would seem that this unknown is lost to us forever. There is no place in the outer world where the *unknown* can be found, for the outer world is always a world *known* from the outside, classified and plastered with labels. It is a world of surfaces, and every attempt to look inside, to take it apart, merely leads to more surfaces. Like a dissected onion, the outer world turns out to be surfaces within surfaces within surfaces, until we are confronted with "indivisible" particles—more surfaces—or "waves of energy" that vanish with their secret. If we could at least *find* this unknown we might be able to wrest free its secret, or experience it; but no tool yet invented by science or philosophy or traditional Christianity has discovered the way to knowledge of this great unknown. The very phrasing of the problem precludes us from it.

But Western man has been so preoccupied with the kind of knowledge that can be expressed in words that he has largely overlooked the possibility of any other. He has thus neglected the knowledge of the mystics gained through direct experience of the unknown, and universally described as ineffable—unspeakable, too sacred for utterance. Mystical experience, when set down in words, has a paradoxical and cryptic form, a symbolic and metaphorical style that baffles the logical mind. The so-called knowledge of the mystic turns out to be, in the mind of the tough-minded Westerner, more like "no-knowledge." Yet the knowledge of the mystic is precisely that knowledge about the unknown which is totally outside the definition of "knowledge" accepted by empirical science. But the fact is that the final understanding of the unknown, the hidden dimension, the beyond in our midst, depends on precisely this unscientific "no-knowledge."

The problem has been phrased this way for a purpose, for it points to the radically different approach to be found in Oriental philosophy. Thus, it is a cardinal principle of Chinese Taoism and Japanese Buddhism that

> He who knows does not speak.
> He who speaks does not know.[2]

Running through the whole of Taoist thinking is the awareness of this apparent contradiction, a paradox that is aptly illustrated in a number of Chinese concepts. The proper kind of action in Taoism is *wu-wei,* "nonaction," the closest analogue of which in Western thinking is the concept of government by the principle of *laissez faire.* Following this pattern, Taoist philosophy contends that the proper way of living is to have *wu-hsin,* "no-mind," or *wu-nien,* "no-thought," which results in the kind of knowledge that can be termed "no-knowledge." The way of

Chinese philosophy is to act without acting, think without thinking, know without knowing, and is perhaps best understood as a way of living spontaneously, without giving it too much thought. To know without knowing is, in fact, the way of the East, and the three great Oriental religions of Hinduism, Buddhism, and Taoism boil down to this strange way of doing things. Moreover, this paradoxical form of knowledge underlies the whole mystical tradition, Oriental and Occidental. It forms the basic type of experience at the heart of the so-called *philosophia perennis,* the Perennial Philosophy, which finds the "same essentially indescribable Fact"[3] underlying *all* religions of the world: the final reality of the universe, though unknown in the sense of factual or discursive knowledge, can nevertheless be known through direct experience.

Hinduism, Buddhism, and Taoism alike agree that the key to the universe is found within our-selves. Outside ourselves we can only confront the universe, but within ourselves we *are* the universe. From this point of view, man is the universe experiencing—feeling what it is like to be a man. Thus the Hindu approach to the innermost shrine of the universe is through the inner quest of man's own identity, the final question being, Who am I?

A little introspection soon reveals that "I" am not a physical body, since I can view my physical being with almost total objectivity. My body is a collection of knowns, even if the mechanics and biochemistry of it are not known intimately by me. It is something tangible, visible, measurable—but not the real "I." Psych-ology, the "science of the soul," leads me no closer to the answer of who "I" am, for the psyche, consisting of ideas and images, desires and concepts and understandings, is still a collection of knowns. None of the ideas of the psyche can really be "I," since "I" am able to *know* these ideas, and therefore they are not "I." What I call "I" is an identity that seems to stand behind my physical, emotional, and mental being. The public image in the minds of my friends and the private image in my own mind are likewise not "I," for they are always constructed out of known facts and ideas about myself that are garnered from my past experiences, behavior, or accomplishments. Yet it is precisely this public image which is mourned by my friends when I die, and it is precisely this private image which I fear to lose and which I protect with all my strength. What am I protecting? Certainly not "I." What I am protecting is my psyche, my soul, a set of ideas and feelings. Thus the cry of the doomed sailor is always SOS, "Save our *souls*." The popular belief in the immortality of the soul is certainly not Biblical; it is rather the Spirit that survives (cf. Eccl. 12:7; John 3:13).

Ultimately, "I" am neither a body nor a soul: "I" am that which *has* a body and a soul. Whatever is known about me by my-self or others is only possessed; but who is the possessor? Every time I think I know who "I" am, there turns out to be another "I" who is doing the thinking and knowing. Ultimately, there seems to be only one possible conclusion: the "I" for which I am searching is the subjective knower who cannot become the object of its own knowledge. It is obvious, then, that "I" can never know who "I" am.

This awareness of the inner "I" that can never be known was reached by Indian philosophers centuries before the dawn of the Christian era. Thus we read in the Upanishads:

Turiya [Pure Consciousness] is not that which is conscious of the inner (subjective) world, nor that which is conscious of the outer (objective) world, nor that which is conscious of both, nor that which is a mass of consciousness. . . . It is unperceived, unrelated,

incomprehensible, uninferable, unthinkable, and indescribable. . . . This is Atman, and this has to be
realized.[4]

In short, the inner "I" (*atman*) cannot be described in
terms of anything that is known. Every time we attempt
such a description, it retreats before us: as the Upanishads
put it, *Neti neti*—"Not this, not that."[5] For the mind can
never formulate a rational idea of what transcends reason
—pure consciousness—any more than light can illumine
itself or fire burn itself.

Empirical science will not accept these conclusions
because they elude the scientific method. The only way to
grasp their meaning is, again, through metaphor. The
comparison of the inner "I," *atman,* to light will clarify
what the mystics have tried to say. Pure light is invisible
and transparent, and therefore essentially indescribable.
But light becomes visible when it falls on objects. Yet light
cannot be described in terms of the shapes and colors that
it illumines, since it is itself shapeless and colorless. Were
it otherwise, light would distort what it illumines, but being
essentially clear, light is able to illumine all shapes and
colors. Pure consciousness is like light. Since it is idea-less,
image-less, and concept-less, it is able to entertain ideas,
images, and concepts; yet it cannot be described in terms
of any of these. Just as light is the object-less ground of
illumined objects, the knower is the un-known ground of
all that is known.

A description of the inner "I" is therefore a kind of
nondescription, just as knowledge of it is "no-knowledge."
But the value of it is precisely this absolute transparency,
just as the value of pots and bowls is not in the visible clay
but in the void they contain. The inner "I" is precisely
that, the container of "things" and "events." In terms of
time, the inner "I" is the container of memory and anticipa-

tion—the past and the future—which are imprinted upon the organism. But these are the *known* traces of awareness; the "I" is awareness itself, the timeless transparency that can dwell in no time at all but *now,* the eternal instant between memory and anticipation. In terms of space, the inner "I" is nowhere and everywhere. And because it is object-less and space-less, it is able to contain the concrete objects of its perception. Being in-finite, it can take in the finite. This is the heart of Hindu religion: "I"—*atman,* Turiya—am infinite consciousness; "I" am one with the "I" of all men and the inner "I" of the universe: *aham brahman,* "I am Brahman."[6] Pure consciousness is man's inner dimension, cutting through space and time, but ultimately indescribable in their terms. "I" am the inside of the universe, the "within" of things. In the words of the *Chhandogya Upanishad:*

> That Infinite, indeed, is below. It is above. It is behind. It is before. It is to the south. It is to the north. The Infinite, indeed, is all this. . . . With reference to "I": "I," indeed, am below. "I" am above. "I" am behind. "I" am before. "I" am to the south. "I" am to the north. "I" am, indeed, all this.[7]

In the words of the Blessed One, Krishna:

> I am the soul self, or *atman,* . . .
> That abides in the heart of all beings;
> I am the beginning and the middle
> Of beings, and the very end too.[8]

Because of the indefinable nature of the inner "I," there is no way to expound its nature logically. At first glance we might reason that a "knower" is the necessary ground for "knowledge" and that an Infinite Knower is the necessary ground for the whole universe of things-which-can-be-known. Yet such an argument is, again, simply the logic of grammar—requiring a "knower" to account for "knowledge," just as it requires a "creator" to account for "creation." Moreover, since Hindu philosophy grew up in an Indo-European culture, the knower-knowledge formula is as completely analogical as the Creator-creation distinction of Christianity—an application of words to the wordless, a tale of the untellable. But, properly understood, the reality behind the analogy, the "I" of all being, can only be apprehended through direct experience and heightened vision.

Modern man would like to *know* this "I"—that is, have it fixed and formulated—just as he would like to have God in a creed or a book. But the Hindu Upanishads make it clear that this is impossible: "That which cannot be apprehended by the mind . . . , that which cannot be perceived . . . , heard . . . , smelt . . . , That alone know as Brahman, and not that [meaning the gods] which people here worship. . . . If you think: 'I know Brahman well,' then surely you know but little of Its form; you know only Its form as conditioned by men or by the gods."[9] Chinese Taoism likewise concurs that the *tao,* the Way of all things, is beyond words. The concept of the *tao* originally meant "speech," so that the opening words of the *Tao Te Ching* begin with a pun: "The Tao that can be *tao*-ed is not Tao," or, as Wing-tsit Chan translates it, "The Tao that can be told of is not the eternal Tao."[10] And, in Mahayana Buddhism, precisely to emphasize the fact that the inner "I" is beyond thought and words, the Self is called *an-atman,* or "not-self." Unable, then, to observe, label, or pin down the "I," we are only able to assert it: *tat tvam asi*—"That art Thou." This we can never under-stand, for it is standing under us, under-grounding our existence like the invisible cord in a string of beads.

In the West there has been a general failure to grasp

the more valuable insights of the East. This has stemmed from a condescending attitude on the part of Christian theologians writing about Eastern philosophy. If there is such a thing as religious snobbery, it has consisted in the tendency to make the Christian God the measuring stick for similar "ultimates" in other religions, and the irritating habit of claiming that our superiority over other religions is obvious—for "Christianity has Christ!" It has thus been far too easy to label Hinduism as "polytheistic," Taoism as "pantheistic," Buddhism as "atheistic," and Zen as "irreligious," or "nonsensical." Westerners have generally defined "religion" from the myopic standpoint of traditional Christian theology, which is a definition based on supernaturalism, that is, mythological dualism understood as fact.

Thus the Christian God has always been the all-powerful Creator, separate from his creation, who produced the world by making (*wei*), like the potter making a pot. Beside this, the Chinese *tao,* producing the world by not-making (*wu-wei*), has seemed puzzling indeed. But in the theology of the "creating" universe the world is not made but *evolved.* The universe is pro-ducing, de-veloping, existing, actually growing out of itself. And the production of the world by *wu-wei,* by "not-making," is very close to the idea of "growing." The God of Christianity, because he made the world, knows it completely, as a mechanic knows his machine. But the *tao,* growing the world from the inside outward, by "not-making," does not know how it is done any more than you know how you grow your hair. For the principle of the *tao* is *tzu-jan,* self-so-ness, naturalness, spontaneous doing, effortless effort. Nothing is so completely relaxed as the *tao,* which effortlessly spawns the whole universe—a concept completely unlike the Creator God who single-handedly commanded the universe into existence like a shouting Cosmic General, tiring himself out so completely during the first week that he had to rest up over the first weekend.

The Hindu idea, too, is that of a universe growing from within. The word "Brahman" derives from the Sanskrit root *brih-*, "to grow, or burst forth," and subsequent derivation suggests something that "gushes forth, overflows, exceeds itself."[11] The "creating" of the world by Brahma, the creative side of Brahma*n*, is thus a growing, bursting forth, or overflowing similar to the effortless growing of the *tao*. The Hindu word for this is *atma-yajna* (self-emptying), which is identical to the *kenosis* of the Godhead in the incarnation, the sacrificial death of the Word in flesh. The Hindu Brahma splits himself asunder, divides his infinite being into finite beings, thus abandoning him-Self in creating the universe. Like the inspired pianist who abandons himself, literally giving himself up to the spontaneous flight of his fingers over the keys, Brahma bursts forth from him-Self, creating the world by Self-immolation, so that the universe is, speaking mythically, his dismembered body.

In another Hindu myth, "creating" takes place through the dreaming of Vishnu the Preserver (another side of Brahma*n*), who goes to sleep and forgets who he is. The world is thus the panorama of his dreaming, a stage populated by his own imagination. Human beings are, therefore, the dreaming Vishnu, forgetting (dis-membering) that he is Vishnu and re-membering only that he is Atman, man's own Self. Thus, *tat tvam asi*, "That art Thou."

The whole universe is therefore a dream of Vishnu, a "trick of illusion," *maya*. The ultimate experience of liberation (*moksha*) in Hinduism is the realization of the world as *maya*, a realization that comes when the Atman of man re-members that it is Brahman. In popular Western understanding, *maya* is usually termed "illusion," an emphasis that was put on the concept in the later Vedantic philosophy. Liberation, from this point of view, means escaping from an illusory and unreal world—an escape that is accomplished by retreating from *maya* into the Self (Atman-Brahman)—thus escaping from the world of suffering, contradiction, pain, and uncertainty. But the world of *maya* is not an "illusion" that must be escaped, but rather one that is to be seen through. For the world that is "made" (*ma*) by *maya* is nature itself, and is related to the Sanskrit words *matra* (element) and *matri* (mother, mother earth, and pl. waters). The ancient Italian earth goddess Maia (for whom our month of May is named) is etymologically related, as is the Latin *mare* (sea) and Old English *mægden* (maiden). In Indo-European languages the words for mother (*māter, mētēr, mère*), along with matter, mass, matrix, meter, and measure, are related to the Sanskrit roots *ma-* and *matri-,* which mean "to measure" or "mark off." The world of *maya* is therefore not only "mother earth" and the "sea," but also the "world as marked off"—that is, the world as divided up or "measured" into finite "things" and "events." Opposed to the world as "illusion," that is, the describable world of measured things and events, is the immeasurable Brahman who is indescribable, unknowable, and beyond words. As R. C. Zaehner puts it, "The 'modifications' of the One True Brahman are . . . verbal distinctions only—transient forms into which the one reality transforms itself, though remaining ever essentially the same."[12] For the creation of the world of separate "things" and "events"—accomplished by the use of words (Let there be light!)—is the "measuring" out of the One Undivided Reality, as when the Word "set a compass upon the face of the depth" (Prov. 8:27, KJV), "separated the light from the darkness" (Gen. 1:4), and established the firmament to "separate the waters from the waters" (v. 6).

The world of *maya,* then, is not to be escaped; indeed, we cannot escape it. For, just as the very ex-isting of Brahman, his "coming out," occurs only when Brahman becomes the world, so too does the ex-isting of my Self— "I" who am Atman-Brahman—occur only when I cease to be "I" and "come out" in the world as a body and a soul. Only then am "I" *real*ized. It is obvious, then, that the doctrine of the "incarnating" Word and the "indwelling" Spirit is precisely the same as the Hindu doctrine, "That art Thou." For the inner "I" or *atman* is more than simply the "self" of man. Ultimately it derives from the Sanskrit root *an-,* "to breathe." Thus *atman*—related to the Greek *atmos,* "vapor," and *autmē,* "breath," "wind"—is also the "breath of life": the *ruach Adonai,* "the breath of the Lord," breathed into man by God (Gen. 2:7). *Atman,* therefore, is that pneumatic principle embodied in the Holy Spirit (*spiritus,* "breath, spirit"; *spirare,* "breathe, be alive") which was breathed by the risen Lord on his disciples (John 20:22) and which came as a "mighty wind" to *in-spire* them on the day of Pentecost (Acts, ch. 2). The Spirit of God (Brahman) is therefore the spirit of man (Atman). In the final Biblical and Upanishadic doctrine of God (the "indwelling" Spirit and Atman-Brahman) is revealed the *philosophia perennis,* the final truth of all religion and all advanced science: that the deepest dimension of man is one with the deepest dimension of the whole universe.

By failing to develop the doctrine of the Spirit, theology has failed to develop the idea of spiritual man—man as made up of body, soul, *and spirit.* Christianity has traditionally viewed man as a duality of body and soul, and therefore spirit has been confused with soul. Only as a

Spirit, as the timeless inner "I," can man discover eternal life "in the Spirit." But when man confuses the Spirit with his own soul, he becomes a purely physical and psychic being confined to temporal existence. From the standpoint of the soul, eternal life becomes a matter of having more and more "time," everlasting life for the personal ego. Thus, by confusing Spirit with soul, theology has destroyed man's link with the Holy Spirit, for when the Spirit is not dis-tinguished from the soul the awareness of one's own divinity is, as it were, ex-tinguished.

The confusion of the Spirit with the soul is one of the unwritten chapters of the history of theology. Paul apparently understood the Spirit as the inner "I" who could know but never be known. "For what person knows a man's thoughts except the spirit of the man which is in him? . . . The *psychic* man does not receive the gifts of the Spirit of God, for [since they are indescribable and unknown] they are folly to him, and he is not able to understand them because they are spiritually discerned. The spiritual man [the inner "I"] judges [i.e., discerns] all things, but is himself to be judged [discerned] by no one. 'For who has known the mind of the Lord [who is Spirit] so as to instruct him?' But we have the mind of Christ [i.e., the Spirit]." (I Cor. 2:11, 14–16.) And again: "The first Adam became a living *soul;* the last Adam [Christ] became a life-giving spirit." (I Cor. 15:45.) For Paul, the way to eternal life was quite clear. One had to rise above being merely a psychic or soul-centered being and become a spiritual being, which meant "eternal life in Christ" (Rom. 6:23). "Put off your old nature which belongs to your former manner of life and is corrupt through deceitful lusts [that is, put off your psychic nature], and be renewed in the spirit of your minds, and put on the new nature, created after the likeness of God." (Eph. 4:22–24.) (The

translations *soul* [*psychē*] and *psychic* [*psychikos*] are my
own, since the KJV, RSV, and NEB translations are badly
misleading.)

Later theology has generally confused spirit and soul,
as did Thomas Aquinas. On the one hand, he identified
the soul with the intellect, which he described as an "in-
corporeal" principle that "can know all corporeal things"
but "cannot have any of them in its own nature, because
that which is in it naturally would impede the knowledge
of anything else."[13] But this description of the *soul* is really
of the *spiritual* knower, which transcends the objects of
its own knowledge. On the other hand, Aquinas makes the
intellect a power of the soul, such that it is able to know its
own character, that is, know the knower. His "intellect"
is, therefore, a complete confusion of soul and spirit. And,
when spirit is confused with the soul, man's divinity is lost
—or, rather, projected to the Godhead. Thus Aquinas says
that "there must needs be some higher intellect, by which
the soul is helped to understand. . . . The separate intellect,
according to the teaching of our Faith, is God Himself, who
is the soul's Creator. . . . Therefore the human soul derives
its intellectual light from Him."[14]

This confusion, by dragging the spirit down to the level
of the soul, has made any assertion of man's divinity appear as pure nonsense. Such a claim appears to be exalting
man's ego rather than his spirit, thus setting up the ego of
man as divine. Moreover, the assertion of man's divinity
clashes with our concept of a God who is primarily transcendent. He may also be immanent, but not in man's ego!
But, to identify God with man's spirit is not to destroy his
transcendence, for transcendence means that God is "beyond" in precisely the sense that he can never become the
object of knowledge, because he is the subjective Knower.
He is not an objective center *to* which we must be related,

like the God of heaven surrounded by his choirs. He is the
subjective Center *with* which man is already related. And
it is only as man's Spirit, and as the Spirit at the heart of
all being, that God ceases to be peripheral and becomes
central. Moreover, to imagine that "I" am anything-apart
from God is to fall into the very pride of Adam. But "I"
am nothing-apart from God precisely because "I" AM
God.

Immediately the cries of "Blasphemy!" go up in all
directions. But this is because the Christian idea of the
I is not the inner "I" but the selfish little ego, the depravity
of which is obvious to all. To call the ego God is blas-
phemous indeed. But there is a world of difference between
saying the ego is God and saying the inner Spirit is God—
between the absurdity of "I am God" and the ultimate
truth that " 'I' am God." For God is the great I AM of the
universe, the authority of which can never be questioned—
unless we would question the Questioner.

The loss of spiritual man has gone hand in hand with
the tremendous development of psychic man—man as a
personal center, a competitive individual, an ego. For
man's ego is precisely that image of himself which has been
called a private or public image: an idea or picture that
he develops before him-Self and before the world. His ego
is not his real Self but a costume or "mask" (*persona*) of
him-Self, the mask of personality. Yet, as much as we
would like to ignore the fact, the doctrine of God depends
very closely on whatever the current doctrine of man is.
Thus the idea of the *Spiritual* God has been largely lost in
the Western world, and in its place has developed the
Psychic God in the image of man's ego. The highest
dimension of the universe is always an extension of the
highest dimension of man himself. Thus, the transcendent
inner "I," mistakenly identified with the *ego* but still felt

as a Presence, has been projected into the heavens as a
supernatural Ego, the Big Ego called God.

The Big Ego of the Old Testament was supplanted in
the New by the kenotic, self-sacrificing God of Love, who
was again replaced by the eternal presence of the "indwelling" Spirit. But, rather than letting the concept evolve,
theology has frozen all three in the static symbolism of the
Trinity. It has therefore never allowed the emergence of
God or man as Spirit, but rather built a theology on the
Old Testament premise that man is pure ego (like Adam)
and God is the Big Ego.

Thus the supernatural God in heaven—the Ruler, the
King, the Lawgiver and Judge—is nothing more than an
overblown Ego. He is "personal" (according to popular
religion), which means he has all the despicable features of
egotistical man. He has the audacity to shout: "I am the
LORD your God . . . . You shall have no other gods before
me. . . . I the LORD your God am a jealous God . . . . You
shall not take the name of the LORD your God in vain . . . .
Let me alone, that my wrath may burn hot against them
and I may consume them . . . . Whoever has sinned against
me, him will I blot out of my book." (Ex. 20:2–3, 5, 7;
32:10, 33.) Against such Divine Pomposity man was
bound to revolt, for such a Boastful Ego is not someone we
want to love or obey but someone we want to obliterate.

As long as God remains a projection of man's own ego,
the Christian condition remains fraught with paradox and
contradiction. For the Big Ego cannot be placated in any
way. He has created us free, yet he *demands* repentance,
obedience, and love. Moreover, every "free" choice we
make is wrong. If man chooses good, the Big Ego takes
the credit, since man is a sinner and therefore can choose
good only by God's grace. If man chooses evil, the Big
Ego passes the buck by condemning man, for God is

"good" and man has been created "free" to choose the good. Man is told he must do good works. If he fails to do them he is damned; yet no number of good works can justify man in the eyes of the Big Ego, who always retorts, like a Big Bully, "That's nuthin'! Look what I've done fer you!" Man is told he must love God. But if man does love God it is *commanded* rather than spontaneous love, and therefore imperfect in the eyes of the Big Ego. To make up for this, man must love God more and more and more: he must love God and praise God and pray for his grace every day, continually confessing imperfect love and begging for one more chance. The ultimate in humiliation will be just right!

Modern religious literature of the "devotional" variety has replaced the Big Ego with a more likable chap—the Nice Guy. God the Father is thus likened to the Great Friend, that most annoying syrupy type who does so many "good" things for you that you are downright embarrassed. This God is the Eternal Porter, the Copilot, or a wonderful Cosmic Pal. All such sentimental conceptions of God are merely more examples of the Big Ego, though he has seemingly learned at last how to win friends and influence people.

The idea of God as the absolutely good Ego leaves man with evil, for which he cannot account. It leaves man with his own rebellious little ego, which refuses to serve the Big Tyrant, leading, naturally, to a huge guilt complex. To save face, man must therefore project another Big Ego, the absolutely Bad Ego who is completely rebellious—the Devil, the dark side of man's own nature incarnate. Man is thus left in the world by himself, torn between two Huge Egos, God and Satan, who try to win him over to their own side. Yet the origin of both the Egotistical God and the Egotistical Devil in the ego of man is perfectly clear, since the battleground between heaven and hell is always waged *in* and *over* man's own soul.

Indian religion never developed the absolute dichotomy between the Good God and the Bad Devil, mainly because it has found the unity of all opposites in the inner "I," that is, Atman-Brahman. Brahman creates the world, including the body and soul of man, by *maya,* by division. Any concept growing out of the soul is therefore necessarily divided. The Good God requires a Bad Devil, since things of the dualistic world are defined by their opposites. But the Hindu One is a fusion of all opposites. Thus, Brahma the Creator and Shiva the Destroyer are aspects of a single ongoing process of "creating-destroying," "living-dying," "gooding-badding," "Godding-Devilling." For this there is no opposite.

The "magic" of the Hindu universe is the *maya* of Vishnu, the sheer imaginative power by which he dreams up the universe of opposites—matter and space, darkness and light, joy and sorrow. Yet, to produce a world of opposites, Vishnu must forget that he is One, dream that he is not Vishnu but rather a whole universe full of created beings, from atoms and stars to ants and elephants and men. Yet every created being shares Atman, so that Vishnu can tread through the universe in a million masks, through a world of good and evil, bliss and suffering, ghettos and palaces, life and death. It is Vishnu, then, who treads the path of creation and destruction, walking through the valley of the shadow of death, and finally dying the agonizing death of man himself. But he does it without fear, for it is all a dream. In the end, after the worst nightmares imaginable—being shipwrecked, hanged, beheaded, crucified, burned in Nazi furnaces, disfigured by napalm—Pop! He wakes up, and remembers that he is Vishnu and it was all a dream. For this is a "resurrecting" universe, and if I die

I can be sure the universe will "I" itself again and again and again.

As long as man's goal in salvation is the preservation of the "persona-lity"—the "mask" of the Spirit—rather than the Spirit itself, he is doomed to dwell in a world of terror and contradiction. His soul will not only remain the battleground of Good and Evil, but he will also delude himself with the impossible dream of eliminating suffering, crime, inequality, war, poverty, and—yes, even death— imagining that the dark side of life will someday disappear. Failing to see him-Self as "indwelling" Spirit, he will project this Presence into the sky, and the projected Big Ego can never be satisfied. Every attempt to get himself into the good books with this God is merely the selfishness of his own ego and therefore impossible before the Big Ego who demands humility. He will go to church to make his peace, not knowing that he carries God into church in his own Spirit. It is an impossible game, for the Self, unaware of it-Self, is trying to find it-Self, imagining it is separate from it-Self, trying to bridge an imaginary gap between itself and it-Self. It all turns into a frustrating game with the Big Ego, an everlasting game of Monopoly with man's ego and the Big Ego trying to "monopolize" the whole scene. And, of course, He wins. Round and round man goes, striving to gain some ground by every possible means —Bible-reading, church donations, Christian "service," prayer groups and retreats and Wednesday worship. But there is no way to win unless it is all seen as a game. And the Big Ego will prevent that if he can, for if man tries to bow out of the game, he will be called a cop-out or a sinner, pridefully running his own life instead of letting the Big Ego run it for him.

Ultimately, religion that strives is based upon false assumptions. To pray to God, worship God, or study God is to *confirm him* as the separate Ego. To try to bridge the gap between our-Selves and God is to assume that there is a gap. To try to unite our being to the being of God is to miss the fact that they are already one. To try to attain eternal life is to miss the fact that it is already ours. For every prayer, every word spoken, every move made by man, is made by the inner "I," who is the Spirit itself. I cannot pray to, communicate with, or join myself to the Spirit, for the Spirit and "I" are one and the same. Every prayer of mine is the Spirit "praying" (Rom. 8:26), every attempt of mine is the Spirit "attempting," every move of mine is the Spirit "moving."

Religion, then, is not a matter of doing things to gain God, reach God, or coerce God. For nothing that can be done can accomplish what has already been accomplished: the total union of man's Spirit with the Spirit of God. Eternal life is therefore not to be won or attained, as if it were not here now. In point of fact it is here, now, precisely because it is life in the here and now, the timeless moment. What needs to be done, then, is to give up myself as an ego and dis-cover and real-ize my Self as the inner "I" who is Atman-Brahman—the Spirit. For when I know who "I" am, I discover that I AM, and also discover who "God" is—the Big Ego of a bygone era. And, once I dis-cover that "I" am *it,* I will no longer be "on fire" with religion, for the way to play the "magic" of this world is to play it "cool," just as Vishnu keeps his head during the worst of his bad dreams.

10
Dancing It

There is "no-time" in the present moment to freeze the world, for that is the "time-less" moment of constant change. From this *point* of view, the separation of space into "things" and time into "events" is di-vision, rather than vision itself. For when we simply "observe and describe" what is going on, the world turns out to be a place of HAPPENINGS, EVENTINGS, FUSINGS, and PAT-TERNINGS. Moreover, since every now brings forth the new, vision reveals a CREATING, DESTROYING, RE-CREATING universe, a constant BEING that is ever BECOMING. Such a vision is full of Mystery, for every new now is EM-BODYING and IN-CARNATING a Mystery beyond belief. This Mystery is the hidden dimen-sion: the "I" of my being, the Center of all being, the IN-DWELLING Spirit.

All of religion is an expression of this Mystery: The whispered wonder or trembling fear of *"Mana! Wakanda! Orenda!"* The dazzling lives of Olympian gods and god-desses. The dis-membering of Brahma and the dreaming of Vishnu. The descent of the Dove. Whitehead describes it this way:

Religion is the vision of something which stands be-yond, behind, and within, the passing flux of im-

mediate things; something which is real, and yet
waiting to be realized; something which is a remote
possibility, and yet the greatest of present facts; something that gives meaning to all that passes, and yet
eludes apprehension; something whose possession is
the final good, and yet is beyond all reach; something
which is the ultimate ideal, and the hopeless quest.[1]

To "speak in secular fashion of God" is to describe this
vision, which is an in-Spiration in itself.

Yet a question remains. To have the "incarnating"
universe described, explicated from the Bible, and defined
in scientific terms is one thing; to experience it is another.
If this secular God talk remains as an experiment, as
simply a new pattern of words rather than a transforming
vision, then it is merely one more verbal trap. It must,
finally, be put to the test of actual, living realization: it
must be experienced. For all theologies, creeds, myths,
symbols, and books are merely guidelines to the living experience. The question is, then, What are we to do about
it? What does the "incarnating" universe demand of us?
How can we experience it? What are we to believe about
it? How do we discover the mysterious "I" that is one with
the Spirit of all things? How do we acquire union with this
Center?

It should be apparent that this vision has nothing to do
with the "mighty acts of God," but rather it concerns the
might "acting." It points to what the universe is doing,
what happens rather than what happened, what *is* rather
than what has been or will be. This DOING is known
only in the present moment, the only moment when "knowing" can take place. This vision of the timeless moment is
precisely that change which comes "in a moment, in the
twinkling of an eye" (I Cor. 15:52), bringing eternal life.

To ask what we are to do is, then, a meaningless question. It implies that we lack something that must be attained, presumably in the future. But the present moment cannot be attained in the future, for it is now. To imagine that we can do something to discover eternal life misses the most obvious fact that we already live that life. The real question is not how we are to attain it but how we could possibly escape it. Perhaps, then, we should ask what we should be doing *in the present moment* to attain eternal life. But again, the question is meaningless, for it assumes that eternal life can be captured in a temporal "doing." But to try to grasp eternal life through temporal action is as foolish as trying to grasp the infinite in a concrete symbol. The name for it is idolatry.

Here, in a word, is the fallacy of the whole concept of "religion" as it is generally practiced. The very idea that one should set aside *a time* for "religion"—for private prayer, a half hour of Bible-reading, an annual weekend "retreat," the weekly hour of worship—or feel the usual guilt if one fails to do so, is based on an idolatrous view of time. Worship itself is not idolatrous, but the worship one *must* do because the church community demands it, or the worship one *should* do because one's conscience says so, is sheer idolatry. For an hour is an "image" of the eternal in the same way that a brass idol is an "image" of the infinite. The hour that *must* be set aside for "religion" is an hour set up as superior to other hours, excluding other hours, and becomes a barrier to the eternal that is found in every hour. Indeed, the very "historical" nature of Christianity, which exalts certain temporal "events" to eternal importance, is a subtle kind of idolatry.

Once it is seen that the "thing which *must* be done" leads directly into idolatry, it becomes apparent that the whole idea of working at religion is basically misguided. The man who works at religion to achieve a state called "salvation" becomes enslaved to an enterprise. "Salvation" becomes one thing among many that is exalted to supremacy, and is therefore idolatrous.[2] Religion, as "something to be done" so that man attains something that is not yet his—knowledge of God, the beatific vision, mystical union, *nirvana*—leads into the most insidious kinds of idolatry, for it is based on the false idea that this "thing to be attained" will contain the divine. But all experiences, visions, or feelings merely point to the divine. To work for them is to work for the wrong thing.

It would seem that to do something to attain eternal life is totally wrong. The obvious conclusion, then, is that we should in fact do nothing, but simply wait for it. Yet waiting for eternal life turns out to be equally wrong, for it assumes and implies that eternal life is not here but in the future. We are back where we began, for whether we do something or do nothing to attain it we are pursuing altogether the wrong course. Eternal life is here and now and nowhere else.

Liberation from the temporal into eternal life comes when we stop trying to attain it, when we stop doing something and stop doing nothing to get it, when we stop looking for the hour when the divine will appear. The hour of eternity is always with us in the timeless moment, right *now,* so short we cannot hold it, so long we cannot escape it. No hour is *more* eternal, no *event* is more religious than another. In the moment when we let go of all attempts to find it, we discover that it has found us. We see that there is nothing to do or not to do, except exactly what we are *doing.* To look anywhere else is a wasteful futility, like riding on an ass in search of a donkey.

But anything so ridiculously obvious is immediately suspect. Modern man is so accustomed to the involuted argument of the philosopher or moralist—the "logical"

proof that takes a hundred distinct steps—that he cannot
grasp anything so absurdly simple. Thus, instead of living
the life that is eternal life, he wants a *method* for living it,
failing to see that real living has no method. What is the
method for seeing the moon, smelling a rose, or tasting
cold water? Most people will say that one must go outside
at night, find a garden, or turn on the tap; but they are
wrong, for these are methods for seeing or smelling or tasting that is to take place in a few seconds, not *now*. When
the actual living situation of seeing, smelling, or tasting is
here, there is no method that we can follow. We just do it.
Life is as simple as that. To make life into a method is to
freeze its movement, or to talk about what is to come. To
try to grasp at life is to lose it. For life is like a giant moving river, large as the Indus, Nile, or Mississippi—real,
flowing water. To pick it up is not only to still its flow but
to find it slipping through the fingers. The thing to do is
not to pick it up but to jump in.

If we cannot do anything to attain eternal life, since
it is already attained, then what are we to believe about it?
What explanation of the world will help us to live this
eternal now? What is to be our statement of faith? But
again, these questions turn out to be meaningless. For no
explanation, belief, or statement of faith can bring us
closer to what is here now. We have already been brought,
or rather, we were never away. Moreover, any theological
explanation or religious confession about the world must
necessarily be based on our experience of the world; but it
must always be the experience of the *past*—an hour ago,
or last week. All Christian confessions of belief, statements
of faith, or theological doctrines, even if based on personal
religious experience, are nevertheless statements built on
past experience. No explanation, no system, no belief, has
ever been built upon the present moment that *is,* right

now; such a moment is always past before the statement is complete. In short, there is absolutely nothing to believe, nothing to be said, nothing to be accepted, *about* this living experience. What is to be accepted is the experience itself.

The theology of the "incarnating" universe does not consist of an explanation, a statement of faith, or a dogmatic belief that must be accepted. It consists rather of a description of the experienced world before our eyes as it *is,* not as it has been, may be, or hoped to be. Such a theology is beyond belief or unbelief, for it requires simply that we look and see. To deny that it is "incarnating" is merely to quarrel over semantics; such a denial means simply that the *word* "incarnating" does not portray the mystery that is seen. This theology is, then, the most undogmatic theology possible, open-ended enough to include the jazz and throb of beat music, the surrealism of modern art, the poetry of Allen Ginsberg or Lawrence Ferlinghetti, the new life-styles of youth on the road and the hippies, and man's newest walk—on the moon—as part of the creative advance of the "indwelling" Spirit. This is the theology of experience.

Again, a dead end seems to have been reached. What sort of religion is this if it has no explanations, beliefs, or creedal statements of faith? But before such a question is answered, another must be asked: What sort of religion is it that *has* explanations, beliefs, and creeds? Such a re-ligion is quite literally one which "binds back" (*re-ligare*), ties us down to words about reality rather than to reality itself. The explanations contained in such a religion are ridiculous, since every particle of dust and every living cell contains a Mystery beyond the power of the human mind. Its statements of faith imply that something must be accepted before man can accept life itself. And finally, such a religion ties down the very activity of the "indwelling" Spirit within us, who manages things regardless of our belief or unbelief.

But the original question still is not answered: How in fact am I to live in the "incarnating" universe? If "I" am already living in it, perhaps I merely need to realize that I am "I," the "indwelling" Spirit. Perhaps this knowledge or realization ought to be my goal.

But immediately it must be asked, *"Whose* goal is it?" When I say that I need to know who I am, do I mean that my *ego* needs to realize it, or do I mean *I* need to realize it? There is a difference. For if the ego needs to realize it, then this need is merely one more selfish, egotistical desire —and realization is merely going to confirm this egoism. I will end up calling myself God, and being proud of it because I will be calling my *ego* God. But the fiction that "I" am an ego is the confusion of Spirit and soul and is precisely that illusion that realization is supposed to correct.

On the other hand, if it is the inner "I" that needs to realize that "I" am "I" then "I" am certainly lost in a most confusing circle. "I" am in need of "I." "I" am chasing "I." The whole thing becomes an impossible game that "I" play with "me," like the child who talks to it-Self as if the Self were someone else. It becomes apparent that there is no need to know the inner "I"—no need to find it, discover it, or realize it—for it is always the inner "I" who is doing the finding, discovering, and realizing. To think otherwise is to be tied to the ego, as if it is the ego rather than "I" doing these things. In short, the inner "I" cannot be reached, because it is always the Reacher; cannot be known, because it is always the Knower; cannot be "eyed," because it is always "I-ing."

Once it becomes apparent that there is nothing to be done, nothing *not* to be done, nothing to believe in, no method of attainment, no possible realization to reach, no explanations to comprehend—the way is clear. No amount of trying or struggling can make us "religious." All of the activities of the church, all of the orthodox religious practices are just so much dead wood when it comes down to the way of the "incarnating" universe and the "indwelling" Spirit.

Long ago the Chinese philosophers realized the absolute futility of *trying,* not only in religion but in every area of life. For trying is inherently against the way of nature, the *tao,* which never tries at anything. The *tao* produces the universe by growing it from the inside outward, not knowing how it is done but never faltering in the doing. Thus the universe grows by the principle of *wei wu wei,* "doing without doing," growing without striving to grow. The *tao* of nature is pure spontaneity, for as Lao-tzu said of the *tao*:

> It accomplishes its task, but does not claim credit
>   for it.
> It clothes and feeds all things but does not claim
>   to be master over them.
>
> Tao invariably takes no action [*wu wei*],
>   and yet there is nothing left undone.[3]

For the Taoist, the way of living is the way of nature, sheer effortless effort, pure spontaneous action. But when we think about it, this is precisely the way the inner "I" already operates when it is left alone. Thus the eye can take in a thousand books on the shelf or myriads of pebbles on the shore at a single effortless glance, without being "stopped" by one. In the single, undivided moment of pure awareness, all things are fused together in the Spirit. At the level of intellect, explanation, belief, or language, the world collapses into a heap of fragments; but in the moment of clear awareness and spontaneous action the world is grasped in its absolute wholeness. Contrary, then, to the usual way of thinking, effort is what destroys experience, for it is against the way of nature itself, which is why the best performers, dancers, skiers, divers, and skaters are always the most relaxed.

The way of life, then, is that of the *tao* which "takes no action." "The *tao*'s principle is *tzu-jan*," which means naturalness, spontaneity, or self-so-ness. The human equivalent of this is "no-mind" (*wu-hsin*) and "no-thought" (*wu-nien*), which means that the proper way of living is to have "no-mind" and "no-thought." R. G. Sui calls this having "no-knowledge" as distinct from the state of ignorance, "having-no" knowledge.[4] The knowing and seeing proper to the *tao* are, then, "knowing without knowing," "seeing without seeing." This is likely to remain a hopelessly insoluble method until one grasps the fact that "knowing without knowing" is sheer *knowing*—with nothing "known" and no "knower." "Seeing without seeing" is pure *seeing;* "experiencing without experiencing" is just *experiencing.* Just as the universe is "creating," with no "Creator" or "creation," man in the act of seeing is pure *seeing,* with no "seen" and no "See-er." And thus it becomes apparent that there is no "I" apart from I-ING— man SEEING, HEARING, FEELING, EXPERIENCING, KNOWING. Thus, even the Spirit, the inner "I" itself, is revealed to be a fiction, a linguistic plug for the subject slot of our grammar. In the moment of giving my-Self up to the here and now of pure awareness, "I" am found—in awareness itself. If I talk about it, I am talking about the past, and dualism pops up again, but in the moment of having it there is only HAVING. In this moment, life is LIVING, with "no-mind" as to how it is done.

Perhaps the perfect crystallization of the technique of "no-mind" and "no-thought" is found in later Chinese philosophy—Chan Buddhism (Zen in Japanese). The peculiar power of Zen stems from the fact that it begins where all other philosophies and religions leave off. Zen itself is neither religion nor philosophy, since it has no God or church, no creeds, rites, or beliefs, and thus no particular philosophical hang-up. For the Chinese and Japanese have known for centuries that

> It cannot be attained by mind;
> It is not to be sought after through mindlessness.
>
> It cannot be created by speech;
> It cannot be penetrated by silence.[5]

Zen is not a "historical" religion but a timeless truth. Thus R. H. Blyth writes that "in so far as men *live* at all, they live by Zen. Wherever there is a poetical action, a religious aspiration, a heroic thought, a union of the nature within a man and the Nature without, there is Zen."[6]

The way of living in the "incarnating" universe is precisely that way which is taught by Zen, though paradoxically there seems to be nothing to teach. For the Buddha is a blade of grass, the substance of belief is the falling leaves of autumn, and the mind is like the footsteps of a bird across the sky. In Zen, enlightenment does not come from studying wise men's words about the universe, for these are so many fingers pointing at the moon. What Zen looks at is the moon itself. Thus, Zen has no scriptures, for *"the Universe is the scripture of Zen."*[7] Whenever a Zen monk asks his Master how to acquire enlightenment, the Master points him back to concrete, living reality. Thus Joshu was once asked by a monk: "What is the meaning of Daruma's coming from the West?" (In Western terms:

What is the essence of Buddhism?) Joshu's answer was: "The magnolia tree in the garden."[8] T'ung-shan was once asked by a monk, "What is the Buddha?" to which he immediately replied, "Three pounds of flax!"[9] This is the so-called method of "direct pointing" (*chih-chih*), designed to lead the young novice into a "direct seeing into," a moment of spontaneous realization, a perception of the "suchness" (*tathata*) of the world which cannot be explained. And, if the novice resists *looking*—if he turns to abstraction, intellectual analysis, or verbal gymnastics—he is likely to learn of the "suchness" of the world very quickly, when his Master whacks him across the shoulders with his ever-ready staff.

The same method is used again and again by the Zen Masters. Their answer is always a variation on one theme: "Get awakening yourself! Then you'll know what it is." This is what the Japanese call *jiyū* (Chinese *tzu-yu*), "self-reliance," and *jizai* (*tzu-tsai*), "self-being." In simpler terms, if you want to know the taste of water, don't ask. Taste it. For ultimate truth is found in ordinary things; as Gudo Kokushi said,

> From the very beginning, the Buddha truth is
>   nothing strange to us:
> Drinking tea, eating rice, and putting on clothes.[10]

"Your everyday life, that is the Tao," said Joshu, and when asked what this meant he replied, "When you are hungry you eat, when you are thirsty you drink, when you meet a friend you greet him."[11] Precisely because eternal life is now, and not something *to be* done, whatever one happens to be *doing* is it.

"What is Zen?"

"Walk on!"[12]

When one learns to live this way, taking the world as

it comes, with no attempt to put it into words, conceptualize it, explain it, or capture it, a number of curious things occur. The universe is seen in its utter wholeness. There are no divided realms to relate, no separate "things" and "events," for what is separate is a product of the di-vision of language rather than vision itself. Something like the "self-validating, self-justifying moment" of Maslow's peak-experience occurs. The world is seen as a process—a GOING ON in the instant of "seeing," a moving, living cosmos describable as "creating-destroying-re-creating." There is no cause and effect, no before and after, no there and then, but only here and now—HERE-ING and NOW-ING. There is no division between "I," the Knower, and the outer world, the known: Knower and known dissolve into "knowing"; See-er and seen collapse into "seeing." Man and nature and God merge with the One which is "All-ing." The abstract knowledge that man is part of his environment, that plants are linked to sunlight, that nature is a seamless robe, becomes the substance of experience. The sacred is found in the secular, the holy in the common, the beyond in our midst.

In the "nick of time," when the world is seen this way, enlightenment has come, or, as the Japanese call it, *satori*. Though *satori* is ultimately beyond words and can only be experienced, it is exactly that experence of the "incarnating" universe which has been described. Ruth Fuller Sasaki describes this world from the Zen point of view as follows:

Zen holds that there is no God outside the universe who has created it and created man. God—if I may borrow that word for a moment—the universe, and man are one indissoluble existence, one total whole. Only THIS—capital THIS—is. Anything and everything that appears to us as an individual entity or

phenomenon, whether it be a planet or an atom, a
mouse or a man, is but a temporary manifestation of
THIS in form; every activity that takes place, whether
it be birth or death, loving or eating breakfast, is but
a temporary manifestation of THIS in activity . . . .
The man of Zen is clearly aware that he is abiding in
and will eternally abide in, THIS AS IT IS; that the
world in which he is living his everyday life is indeed
THIS in its myriads of manifestations, forever changing, forever transforming, but forever THIS.[13]

Man "abiding in" THIS AS IT IS: man "dwelling in"
Spirit. The Spirit is THIS, and THIS is all-that-there-is,
the infinite. To find ourselves abiding in THIS is to discover THIS as "in-dwelling" Spirit. The whole universe
is THIS, the Spirit-in-activity, forever changing, transforming, evolving, but forever THIS—forever "resurrecting." And because I AM, I AM THIS also.

Who am I? What is THIS? These questions are so difficult, and yet they are the same question. Why, when we
are confronted with THIS at every turn, is it so hard to
find? Precisely because we have forgotten that the whole
universe is THIS, just as I have forgotten that I am "I."
In the same way that "I" have allowed myself to become a
host of other things—an ego, a persona-lity, a picture
dredged up from my past, a physical body—I have allowed
THIS to become a host of "things" and "events," a whole
universe of men and mice and mountains, yesterday, today,
and tomorrow, which I no longer see as THIS. But surely
it is obvious that "I" and THIS could not ex-ist if they did
not cease to be "I" and THIS—if they did not "come out"
as "me" and "this" and "that." For the world is "creating"
by "incarnating," by a mighty Self-abandonment that turns
energetic vibration into solid "stuff," the Self into selves,
no-thing into "things." From atom to galaxy, the universe
is a dancing drama, a perpetual "acting" in which "I" give

myself up to my ego and body, in which THIS gives itself up to the march of a million million billion flaming suns.

To discover the universe as a dancing drama is to unlock the secret of much that puzzles man about himself and his universe. In any drama, the central concern for the producer and audience is the "acting." The point of drama is to forget who is who, so that the identity of the actor is lost. Thus the universe is concerned not with a duality of Creator-creation, but as a unity of "creating." To coldly analyze a play into the actor and the acting is to miss the point, and a play that allows us to so analyze it is a bad play. But when the "actor" disappears into his "acting," he gives him-Self up, and we lose our-Selves in the skill of the "playing," the magic, the art, the illusion, *maya*.

Thus real living is a kind of play. We put on our working clothes to play the workman and our silk gloves to play the snob. Like all good actors, our main concern is always "to create a good impression," "put up a good front," "put the best foot forward," and sometimes "put on the dog." We are all the same (THIS) underneath, but jackets and jeans turn us into doctors or dropouts. We put on our morals whenever we put on our clothes. This is why people are so downright fascinating—we cannot help watching how they will "play their part" or "do their thing." Moreover, insincerity is always a private ego-trip. And so we love to get "dressed up," go to a costume party, or get stoned out of our minds—all so we can forget who we are.

There is always a profound humor in the discovery that life is just an "acting." Policemen are only policemen in police uniforms and look immensely funny at a policemen's beach party. The grand Houdini act, implicit in the energetic designing of the elements, runs through the very fabric of the universe, giving rise to the cops-and-robbers, cowboys-and-Indians games of children, the social games and war games and sports games, the one-upmanship games of the Big Powers and the Big Lie games of those who have to "save face." We never get away from it, for even our leisure time centers on playing games—bridge and baseball and charades.

The best acting is spontaneous "acting without acting," the artless way of nature herself. Wild birds have no mind to cast their reflection, the water does not try to catch their image. Birds and water are there, and do these things, and this is the final Mystery. As Paul Reps wrote beside a simple Zen sketch, "Cucumber unaccountably cucumbering."[14]

The fact of the matter is that we have forgotten how to *see*. We have become so accustomed to the world that we fall into the lazy habit of letting life slip by, or the stupid habit of missing it by trying to figure out how to feel and think about it, rather than looking at it. But, in the moment that thinking comes to an end and pure living begins, the world is re-created before our eyes, by our own looking and doing. For it is our own seeing that creates the rainbow, and our own running that makes the rainbow run. And we are all the time, unwittingly, "sparkling" the stars, "greening" the trees, and "sounding" the wind in the grass.

When THIS is discovered in THIS "creating," and "I" am discovered in THIS "seeing" and THIS "doing," it is one discovering, that is ONE "discovering." The moment comes alive with the most fantastic drama imaginable and the whole universe becomes a dance—THIS "dancing." In a moment it is realized that all the world's a stage. And when we see THIS "dancing" there is nothing left for us to do other than dancing THIS too. Ancient Hindu philosophers had a name for THIS "dancing": they called it *lila,* "play," "sport"—the *"lilt*ing" or "playing" or "sporting" of the One. In Hindu mythology, the whole universe is the One "acting" as Many, Brahma abandoning him-Self to *maya,* Vishnu dreaming he is me, Shiva sporting himself as the world: INCARNATING.

The dance of Shiva as Nataraja, Lord of the Dance, is, as Coomaraswamy pointed out, "the clearest image of the activity of God which any art or religion can boast of."[15] Images of Shiva often show him in the midst of a circle of fire that he himself spins out by his own whirling torch, dancing to an eternal rhythm that he himself is beating on a drum. A million arms are swinging, a trillion eyes are flashing, weaving a web of "magic" (*maya*) all around. The "incarnating" universe is the dancing of Shiva, who is "creating-destroying" it in one complete rhythm. In his fantastic "playing" he weaves a web of pure energy, e-volves the dance of ten billion galaxies, spins out the drama of life. There can never be an end to it all, for the endless knot of the cosmos keeps bulging with a new loop, the dancer keeps inventing a new step. Stars appear like bubbles in the foam, galaxies wheel in the midst of the void, life moves out of the heart of star dust, does its "th-ing," and slips away behind the curtain. This is the "incarnating" universe, the most magnificent frolic imaginable, the go-go dance of all time. How can we tell the dancer from the dance? There is no need—for us there is only the dancing. Then how do we enter the dance? It is the easiest thing in the world, though we persist in asking how. "Come to me," said Jesus, "for my yoke is easy, and my burden is light." (Matt. 11:28, 30.) A young Zen enthusiast once asked his Master, Gensha, how to enter the path of the Buddha. "Do you hear that stream?" asked the Master. "Why yes," answered the student. "There," said Gensha, "is the way to enter."[16]

When we tread that path we find we are just THIS—
DANCING.

Is this "religion"?

If by "religion" we mean something to believe, something to do, or a sacred hour to keep, then this is not
"religion." Whatever religion seeks to reach has not only
been reached—but is doing the reaching.

Is this "Christian"?

In the "incarnating" universe there is no "heaven" or
"earth"—no "Creator" or "creation"—and therefore no
"belief" or "unbelief." This is neither "Christian" nor
"unchristian," neither "true" nor "untrue"—it is just
THIS. There is no "in" group, no "out" group, just THIS
—"grouping."

Is this "Zen"?

We cannot really say, for, as Lao-tzu put it,

> He who knows does not speak.
> He who speaks does not know.[17]

Or, as Suzuki once said: "When I raise the hand thus, there
is Zen. But when I assert that I have raised my hand, Zen
is no more there."[18]

Is it, then, simply the "incarnating" universe?

Yes, provided we do not *say* that this is it. For THIS
is neither "it" nor "this" nor "that." It is just THIS, beyond belief, nothing more. To find THIS, "Walk on!"

NOTES

Chapter 1. God's Death in Our Time

1. Peter L. Berger, *A Rumor of Angels: Modern Society and the Rediscovery of the Supernatural* (Doubleday & Company, Inc., 1969), p. 4.

2. Martin E. Marty, *Varieties of Unbelief* (Doubleday & Company, Inc., 1966), Ch. 6.

3. Philip Leon, *Beyond Belief and Unbelief: Creative Nihilism* (London: Victor Gollancz, Ltd., 1965), p. 53.

4. John A. T. Robinson, *Honest to God* (London: SCM Press, Ltd., 1963), pp. 11 ff.

5. Friedrich Nietzsche, *Thus Spake Zarathustra,* in *The Portable Nietzeche,* tr. and ed. by Walter Kaufmann (The Viking Press, Inc., 1954), p. 124; Julian Huxley, *Religion Without Revelation* (New American Library, Inc., 1957), p. 59; and Thomas J. J. Altizer, *The Gospel of Christian Atheism* (The Westminster Press, 1966).

6. D. R. G. Owen, *Body and Soul: A Study on the Christian View of Man* (The Westminster Press, 1956), p. 124. For a fuller treatment of scientism see Owen's *Scientism, Man, and Religion* (The Westminster Press, 1952).

7. Martin Buber, *I and Thou* (Charles Scribner's Sons, 1958). Cf. also Paul Tillich's distinction between "controlling knowledge" ("I-It") and "receiving knowledge" ("I-Thou") in his *Systematic Theology,* 3 vols. (The University of Chicago Press, 1951–1963), Vol. I, pp. 71–105.

8. Berger, *op. cit.*, p. 49.

9. John Stapylton Habgood, "The Uneasy Truce Between Science and Theology," in *Soundings: Essays Concerning Christian Understanding,* ed. by A. R. Vidler (London: Cambridge University Press, 1963), pp. 21–41.

10. Gabriel Vahanian, *The Death of God: The Culture of Our Post-Christian Era* (George Braziller, Inc., 1961).

11. Howard Eugene Root, "Beginning All Over Again," in Vidler (ed.), *Soundings,* p. 12.

12. Augustine, *The City of God,* Part V, Bk. 21.

13. Harvey Cox, *The Secular City: Secularization and Urbanization in Theological Perspective* (The Macmillan Company, 1965), pp. 3–4.

14. Dietrich Bonhoeffer, *Letters and Papers from Prison* ed. by Eberhard Bethge, tr. by Reginald H. Fuller (London: SCM Press, Ltd., 1953), pp. 122–123.

15. Albert Einstein, "Science and Religion," *Science News Letter,* Sept. 2, 1940, p. 182.

16. Besides Altizer, *op. cit.,* and Vahanian, *op. cit.,* see William Hamilton, *The New Essence of Christianity* (Association Press, 1961), and Paul M. van Buren, *The Secular Meaning of the Gospel: An Analysis of Its Language* (The Macmillan Company, 1963).

17. Antony Flew, in *New Essays in Philosophical Theology,* ed. by Antony Flew and Alasdair MacIntyre (London: SCM Press, Ltd., 1963), p. 97.

18. John A. T. Robinson, Appendix I, "Can a Truly Contemporary Person *Not* Be an Atheist?" *The New Reformation?* (The Westminster Press, 1965), p. 110.

19. Nietzsche, *op. cit.,* p. 294.

20. Robinson, *The New Reformation?* p. 112.

21. The title of a poem by Francis Thompson (1859–1907).

22. Hamilton, *op. cit.,* p. 65.

23. Leon, *op. cit.,* pp. 59 ff.

24. *Ibid.,* pp. 60–61.

25. Benjamin Lee Whorf, *Language, Thought, and Reality: Selected Writings of Benjamin Lee Whorf,* ed. by John B. Carroll (The M.I.T. Press, 1956), pp. 152–153.

CHAPTER 2. THE SEAMLESS ROBE OF NATURE

1. John Dewey and Arthur F. Bentley, *Knowing and the Known* (Beacon Press, Inc., 1949), p. 69.

2. Pierre Teilhard de Chardin, *The Phenomenon of Man* (London: William Collins Sons & Co., Ltd., 1959), p. 32.

3. The most readily available accounts of stellar evolution are Fred Hoyle's *Frontiers of Astronomy* (Harper & Brothers, 1955) and Robert Jastrow's *Red Giants and White Dwarfs: The Evolution of Stars, Planets and Life* (Harper & Row, Publishers, Inc., 1967).

4. Robert C. Cameron, "Stellar Evolution," *Introduction to Space Science,* ed. by Wilmot N. Hess (Gordon & Breach Science Publishers, Inc., 1965), p. 769.

5. Milton K. Munitz, *The Mystery of Existence: An Essay in Philosophical Cosmology* (Meredith Press, 1965).

6. This analysis of the early atmosphere was first set forth by A. I. Oparin, in *The Origin of Life* (The Macmillan Company, 1938). Readily available accounts of this phase of evolution are Irving Adler, *How Life Began* (A Signet Book, New American Library, Inc., 1957); Isaac Asimov, *The Well-Springs of Life* (A Signet Book, New American Library, Inc., 1960); Harold F. Blum, *Time's Arrow and Evolution* (Harper & Row, Publishers, Inc., 1962); and J. H. Rush, *The Dawn of Life* (A Signet Book, New American Library, Inc., 1957).

7. Wendell M. Stanley, "Some Chemical, Medical and Philosophical Aspects of Viruses," *Science,* Vol. XCIII, No. 2407 (Feb. 14, 1941), pp. 150–151.

8. Teilhard de Chardin, *op. cit.,* pp. 43–44.

9. Habgood, *loc. cit.,* p. 27.

CHAPTER 3. ORIGINS IN ANTIQUITY

1. R. M. Hare, in Flew and MacIntyre (eds.), *op. cit.,* pp. 99–103.

2. Alfred North Whitehead, *Science and the Modern World* (New American Library, Inc., 1948), pp. 49 ff.

218   THE MAGNIFICENT FROLIC

3. Robert Redfield, *The Primitive World and Its Transformations* (Cornell University Press, 1953), p. 104.

4. See J. C. Carothers, "Culture, Psychiatry and the Written Word," *Psychiatry*, Nov., 1959.

5. Marshall McLuhan, *The Gutenberg Galaxy* (University of Toronto Press, 1962), pp. 19 ff.

6. See John Wilson, "Film Literacy in Africa," *Canadian Communications*, Vol. I, No. 4 (Summer, 1961), pp. 7–14.

7. Lancelot Law Whyte, *The Next Development in Man* (New American Library, Inc., 1949), p. 30.

8. Teilhard de Chardin, *op. cit.*, pp. 190 ff.

9. Whyte, *op. cit.*, p. 40.

10. Alfred North Whitehead, *Modes of Thought* (Capricorn Books, G. P. Putnam's Sons, 1958), p. 48.

11. Gilbert Ryle, *The Concept of Mind* (Barnes & Noble, Inc., 1949), p. 15.

12. W. M. Urban, *Language and Reality* (London: George Allen & Unwin, Ltd., 1939), p. 181.

13. Robinson, *Honest to God*, p. 13.

14. Ludwig Wittgenstein, *Philosophical Investigations,* tr. by G. E. M. Anscombe (2d ed., The Macmillan Company, 1958), Sec. 66.

CHAPTER 4. A RADICAL EXPERIMENT

1. Susanne Langer, *Philosophy in a New Key: A Study in the Symbolism of Reason, Rite, and Art* (New American Library, Inc., 1948), p. 82.

2. F. Scott Fitzgerald, *The Great Gatsby* (Charles Scribner's Sons, 1925), p. 182.

3. Henry Bettenson (ed.), *Documents of the Christian Church* (London: Oxford University Press, 1943), p. 73.

4. Paul Tillich, "The Immortality of Man," *Pastoral Psychology*, Vol. VIII, No. 75 (June, 1957), pp. 23–24.

5. Henry Thoreau, *The Portable Thoreau,* ed. by Carl Bode (The Viking Press, Inc., 1947), pp. 628, 272.

6. Abraham H. Maslow, *Toward a Psychology of Being* (2d ed., D. Van Nostrand Company, Inc., 1962), p. 79.

7. T. R. Miles, *Religion and the Scientific Outlook* (London: George Allen & Unwin, Ltd., 1959), p. 161.

8. Whorf, *op. cit.*, p. 214.

9. *Ibid.*, p. 240.

10. Aristotle, *Metaphysics,* tr. by John Warrington (London: J. M. Dent & Sons, Ltd., Publishers, 1956), p. 184.

11. Whorf, *op. cit.*, pp. 57–64.

12. *Ibid.*, pp. 51–56.

13. Whyte, *op. cit.*, Preface, pp. 9–12.

14. Whorf, *op. cit.*, p. 243.

15. Alan W. Watts, *Psychotherapy East and West* (Pantheon Books, Inc., 1961), p. 35.

16. Alan W. Watts, *The Book: On the Taboo Against Knowing Who You Are* (Pantheon Books, Inc., 1966), p. 85.

Chapter 5. The Creating Universe

1. Paul Tillich, *The Courage to Be* (Yale University Press, 1952), pp. 186 ff.

2. Henri Bergson, *Creative Evolution,* tr. by Arthur Mitchell (Modern Library, Inc., 1944), p. xix.

3. Langdon Gilkey, *Maker of Heaven and Earth: The Christian Doctrine of Creation in the Light of Modern Knowledge* (Doubleday & Company, Inc., 1965), p. 23.

4. Tillich, *Systematic Theology,* Vol. III, p. 31.

5. *Ibid.*, Vol. II, p. 7.

6. Alan W. Watts, *The Supreme Identity: An Essay on Oriental Metaphysic and the Christian Religion* (The Noonday Press, 1957), p. 68.

7. Alfred North Whitehead, *Process and Reality: An Essay in Cosmology* (Harper & Brothers, 1960), p. 161; see also Eugene H. Peters, *The Creative Advance: An Introduction to Process Philosophy as a Context for Christian Faith* (The Bethany Press, 1966).

8. Norman J. Berrill, *You and the Universe* (Fawcett Publications, Inc., 1959), p. 173.

9. Norman J. Berrill, *Man's Emerging Mind* (Fawcett Publications, Inc., 1955), p. 234.

10. See Alexander Heidel, *The Babylonian Genesis: The Story of Creation* (2d ed., The University of Chicago Press, 1951).

11. See Ernst Cassirer, *The Philosophy of Symbolic Forms*, tr. by Ralph Manheim (Yale University Press, 1955), Vol. II, pp. 73–82. Bibliography, p. 76, n. 2.

12. Ernst Cassirer, *Language and Myth*, tr. by Susanne K. Langer (Dover Publications, Inc., 1946), p. 65.

13. *Ibid.*, p. 66.

CHAPTER 6. THE INCARNATING CHRIST

1. Bettenson (ed.), *op. cit.*, p. 73.

2. Tillich, *Systematic Theology*, Vol. II, p. 139.

3. *Ibid.*, p. 140.

4. Hamilton, *op. cit.*, p. 89. Italics added.

5. Tillich, *Systematic Theology*, Vol. II, p. 94.

6. John Milton, *Paradise Lost*, Book IX, 11. 781–784, 1000–1004.

7. Bonhoeffer, *op. cit.*, p. 179.

8. Meister Eckhart, *Meister Eckhart's Sermons*, tr. by Claud Field (London: Alec R. Allenson, Inc., n. d.), p. 32.

CHAPTER 7. THE INDWELLING SPIRIT

1. Tillich, *Systematic Theology*, Vol. II, p. 156.

2. Werner and Lotte Pelz, *God Is No More* (London: Victor Gollancz, Ltd., 1964), p. 127 n.

3. Tillich, *Systematic Theology*, Vol. II, p. 154.

4. Alan W. Watts, *The Meaning of Happiness* (James Ladd Delkin, 1940), p. 3.

5. Ananda K. Coomaraswamy, "The Darker Side of Dawn," *Smithsonian Miscellaneous Collections*, Vol. XCIV, No. 1 (April 17, 1935), p. 1.

6. Alan W. Watts, *The Two Hands of God: The Myths of Polarity* (George Braziller, Inc., 1963), p. 182.

7. For the evidence for a Pauline chronology, see John Knox, *Chapters in a Life of Paul* (Abingdon-Cokesbury Press, 1950).

8. Athanasius, *De Incarnatione*, Verbi, I, cviii.

Chapter 8.   The Center Beyond Belief

1. William Wordsworth, "The Tables Turned," 1. 28.

2. Ludwig Wittgenstein, *Tractatus Logico-Philosophicus,* tr. by D. F. Pears and B. F. McGuinness (London: Routledge & Kegan Paul, Ltd., 1961), 6.522, 7.

3. D. E. Harding, "The Universe Revalued," *Adventures of the Mind: Third Series,* ed. by Richard Thruelsen and John Kobler (Vintage Books, Random House, Inc., 1959), p. 264.

4. Wittgenstein, *Philosophical Investigations,* Sec. 109.

5. Edmund W. Sinnott, *The Biology of the Spirit* (The Viking Press, Inc., 1957).

6. *Ibid.,* p. 49.

7. *Ibid.*

8. Herbert Spencer Jennings, *The Universe and Life* (Yale University Press, 1933), p. 14.

9. Sinnott, *op. cit.,* p. 133.

10. Teilhard de Chardin, *op. cit.,* p. 56.

11. *Ibid.,* p. 57.

12. J. S. Haldane, *Mechanism, Life and Personality* (E. P. Dutton & Company, Inc., 1914), p. 98.

13. Whitehead, *Science and the Modern World,* p. 105.

14. J. W. N. Sullivan, *The Limitations of Science* (A Mentor Book, New American Library, Inc., n. d.), p. 106.

15. Quoted in Will Durant, *The Story of Philosophy* (Simon and Schuster, Inc., 1954), p. 6.

16. "Mentoid": a word coined by Julian Huxley in his Introduction to Teilhard de Chardin's *The Phenomenon of Man,* p. 16.

17. Paul Tillich, *Systematic Theology,* Vol. III, pp. 11–30.

18. Sir Arthur Eddington, *The Nature of the Physical World* (London: J. M. Dent & Sons, Ltd., 1935), p. 280.

19. Ralph Waldo Emerson, *Emerson's Works* (London: George Routledge & Sons, Ltd., 1903), Vol. II, pp. 253, 275, 286; Vol. I, p. 316.

Chapter 9.   Brahman and Tao

1. Bonhoeffer, *Letters and Papers from Prison,* p. 124.

2. Wing-tsit Chan (tr.), *The Way of Lao Tzu* (The Bobbs-Merrill Company, Inc., 1963), no. 56.

3. Aldous Huxley, "Introduction" to *The Song of God: Bhagavad-Gita,* tr. by Swami Prabhavananda and Christopher Isherwood (New American Library, Inc., 1954), p. 12.

4. Swami Nikhilananda (tr.), *Mandukya Upanishad,* 7, in *The Upanishads* (Harper & Row, Publishers, Inc., 1964); all subsequent Upanishadic quotations are from this translation.

5. *Brihadaranyaka Upanishad,* III.ix.26.

6. *Ibid.,* I.iv.10.

7. *Chhandogya Upanishad,* VII.xxv.1; punctuation ("I") according to V. K. Chari.

8. Franklin Edgerton (tr.), *The Bhagavad Gita* (Harper & Row, Publishers, Inc., 1964), x.20.

9. *Kena Upanishad,* I.6–9; II.1.

10. Chan (tr.), *op. cit.,* no. 1.

11. S. Radhakrishnan (ed. and tr.), *The Principal Upanishads* (London: George Allen & Unwin, Ltd., 1953), p. 52.

12. R. C. Zaehner, *Hinduism* (Oxford University Press, Inc., 1966), p. 53.

13. Anton C. Pegis (ed.), *Introduction to Saint Thomas Aquinas* (Modern Library, Inc., 1948), Q. 75, Art. 2.

14. *Ibid.,* Q. 79, Art. 4.

CHAPTER 10.   DANCING IT

1. Whitehead, *Science and the Modern World,* p. 191.

2. See Hubert Benoit, "The Idolatry of 'Salvation,' " *The Supreme Doctrine: Psychological Studies in Zen Thought* (The Viking Press, Inc., 1959), pp. 15–17.

3. Chan (tr.), *op. cit.,* nos. 34, 37.

4. R. G. H. Sui, *The Tao of Science: An Essay on Western Knowledge and Eastern Wisdom* (The M.I.T. Press, 1964), p. 75.

5. R. H. Blyth, *Haiku* (Tokyo: The Hokuseido Press, 1949), Vol. I, pp. 21–22.

6. R. H. Blyth, *Zen in English Literature and Oriental Classics* (E. P. Dutton & Company, Inc., 1960), p. vii.

7. Ananda K. Coomaraswamy, *Buddha and the Gospel of Buddhism* (Harper & Row, Publishers, Inc., 1964), pp. 254–255.

8. Blyth, *Haiku,* Vol. I, p. 24.

9. Alan W. Watts, *The Way of Zen* (Pantheon Books, Inc., 1957), p. 127.

10. Amakuki Sessan, "Hakuin's 'Song of Meditation,' " *A First Zen Reader,* tr. by Trevor Leggett (Tokyo: Charles E. Tuttle, 1960), p. 189.

11. D. T. Suzuki, *Zen and Japanese Culture* (Pantheon Books, Inc., 1959), p. 11.

12. Christmas Humphreys, *Zen Buddhism* (London: George Allen & Unwin, Ltd., 1961), pp. 62, 170. See also his *Walk On!* (London: The Buddhist Society, 1956).

13. Ruth Fuller Sasaki, "Zen: A Method for Religious Awakening," *The World of Zen: An East-West Anthology,* ed. by Nancy Wilson Ross (Random House, Inc., 1960), pp. 18, 28.

14. *Ibid.,* p. 261.

15. Ananda K. Coomaraswamy, *The Dance of Shiva* (The Sunwise Turn, 1924), p. 56. For a complete explanation of this symbol, see Heinrich Zimmer, *Myths and Symbols in Indian Art and Civilization,* ed. by Joseph Campbell (Harper & Row, Publishers, Inc., 1962), pp. 151–175.

16. D. T. Suzuki, *Studies in Zen* (Delta Publishing Company, 1955), p. 199.

17. See Chapter 9, note 2.

18. D. T. Suzuki, *Zen Buddhism,* ed. by William Barrett (Doubleday & Company, Inc., 1956), p. 129.